"A powerful Dragoon approaching cautiously, came behind McMichael, and with one stroke of his ponderous blade clave his head in two." p. 59.

TRADITIONS

OF

THE COVENANTERS

OR

GLEANINGS AMONG THE MOUNTAINS.

BY THE

REV. ROBERT SIMPSON,

SANQUHAR.

Gather up the fragments that remain, that nothing be lost.

And they overcame him by the blood of the Lamb, and by the word of their testimony; and they loved not their lives unto the death.

PHILADELPHIA:

PRESBYTERIAN BOARD OF PUBLICATION.

CONTENTS.

CHAPTER I.

Page

Sanquhar—Howatson—Hair—Adams, . . . 9

CHAPTER II.

Peden in Glendyne — Woman at Inglestone — Craigdaroch, ... 20

CHAPTER III.

Sanquhar Declaration—Conventicle in Blagannach Moss, 30

CHAPTER IV.

Scar—James McMichael, ... 46

CHAPTER V.

Peden—Castle Gilmour—Auchentagart—Elliock—Glenquhary Cleuch, ... 61

CHAPTER VI.

William Swan—Scene in the Barn—Cave at the Crags—Conventicle at Wardlaw—Search for Arms—Incident, ... 78

CHAPTER VII.

Bellybught—Scene at Auchengrouch—The Pursuit, . 92

CHAPTER VIII.

Muirkirk — John Richard—Thomas Richard—William Moffat, of Hartfell, ... 106

CHAPTER IX.

Durisdeer—Elias Wilson—Adam Clark of Glenim—Muncie, the informer—Mitchelslacks—Michael Smith, of Quarrel Wood, ... 118

CHAPTER X.

Page

Thomas Harkness, Andrew Clark, and Samuel McEwen —Daniel McMichael—Babe of Tweedhope-foot—John Hunter, - - - - - - - - 130

CHAPTER XI.

Thomas Hutchison, of Daljig—Marion Cameron—Margaret Wilson, - - - - - - - 142

CHAPTER XII.

Lesmahagow—Thomas Brown, of Auchlochan—Smith, of Treepod—John Gill—Stobo, - - 153

CHAPTER XIII.

Martyrdom at Crossgellioch—Hugh Hutchison—Campbell of Dalhanna—Hair and Corson—Brown and Morice, - - - - - - - 164

CHAPTER XIV.

Hugh Hutchison—Further particulars, - - - 175

CHAPTER XV.

John Paterson, of Penyvenie, - - - - 186

CHAPTER XVI.

Capture at Glenshilloch—Rescue—Shooting at Craignorth—Roger Dun—James Douglas, - - - 197

CHAPTER XVII.

Story of Alexander Brown. - - - - 207

PREFACE.

THE collection of the following anecdotes respecting our persecuted ancestors was at first purely incidental. The editor of the "Weekly Christian Teacher" having requested of the Author a communication for his miscellany, there was sent to him a paper containing two or three anecdotes, entitled, "Reminiscences of the Covenanters," and after its transmission no more was contemplated. At the further solicitation of the conductor of that periodical, however, a second paper was prepared, and then a third. At length the idea was entertained, that something more than a few stray notices of the worthies of the Covenant might perchance be gleaned in the neighbourhood of the Author's residence, as the locality is well known to have been the frequent resort of the suffering wanderers during the dark and protracted period of the church's affliction in Scotland. The attempt was successful, and resembled the striking of the enchanted ground with the mystic wand, when innumerable *elfins*, formerly invisible, started up all around. The writer, though fully aware that the

1 *

memory of not a few incidents which occurred in these trying times was still retained by the peasantry among the mountains and glens of the district, had yet no idea of the vast number of traditional stories that really existed. Having been made aware of the fact, therefore, his object was to collect and arrange them in the best manner he could, and then to publish them in a series of articles.

The sources from which these anecdotes are drawn are chiefly the descendants of the persons themselves to whom the incidents refer. They have been retained as heir-looms in the families of the worthy men who suffered so much in the cause of truth and righteousness. This circumstance affords a strong guaranty for the fidelity and correctness of the transmission. The traditions of that persecuting period, especially when we consider the channel through which they have been conveyed, may be pretty safely relied on. Absolute correctness, like that of historic narration, is not to be expected; still the anecdotes are veritable and substantially accurate, although some attendant circumstances may probably in the lapse of three generations have varied in the telling. They are all of them precisely in keeping with the times to which they refer. In some cases the same anecdote has been communicated by different persons in places widely separate, and yet the story with a slight variation was exactly the same—further proof that the traditions are, in the main, faithful. It would seem, however, from the complexion of many of them, that the occurrences related took place mostly after the *seventy-nine*, the year of Drumclog and Bothwell, and of the Archbishop's death, the consequent severities of which were heightened by the Sanquhar Declaration, and the skirmish at Airds-moss.

The locality which it has been attempted to glean, is *that* chiefly in the midst of which Sanquhar is situated, assuming this place as a centre, and stretching out in a radius of twenty or thirty miles in extent on all sides. It was to this locality, as Wodrow informs us, that great numbers of the wanderers from the more level and exposed parts of the country resorted. "Multitudes," says the historian, "were hiding and wandering in mountains and caves, and not a few from other places of the kingdom had retired to the mountainous parts of Galloway and Nithsdale."

The volume now presented to the public contains a few only of the anecdotes that are at this day extant in the district to which the researches have been chiefly confined, and are merely a *part* of those which are in the possession of the writer, the rest being in the mean time withheld, lest the volume should become too bulky, and too expensive for the persons for whose benefit it is principally intended.

In furnishing this series of anecdotes, the author may remark, that he has in no instance used an unwarranted freedom with any of them. It was found necessary occasionally to correct dates, and slightly to alter a few collateral circumstances, but in no case has the main incident been meddled with. He has used full liberty, where it was legitimate to do so. He has occasionally attempted to depict the local scenery; in some cases he has supposed circumstances in keeping with the verisimilitude of the story, such as the meditative mood of the venerable Peden at the mouth of the dark Glendyne, on a fine summer day, when all nature was jocund around him; and similar things in other places, where, in the absence or default of tradition, the imagination is left to picture the seeming reality. He has endeavoured to put flesh and skin upon the dry bones of bare incidents, by making here and there what he conceived to be an appropriate remark; and he has adverted to the history of the period, when by that means any additional light could be cast on the subject of the anecdote in hand.

R. S.

TRADITIONS

OF

THE COVENANTERS.

CHAPTER I.

Sanquhar—Howatson—Hair—William Adams.

In no part of our native land, perhaps, did the fires of persecution rage with a fiercer flame than in the south-west of Scotland. The higher district of Nithsdale, where it joins the upper ward of Lanarkshire, was especially, at certain periods of the oppressive reign of the second Charles, a scene of tragical interest. The locality in the midst of which the ancient burgh of Sanquhar is situated, was the theatre of many an act of persecuting violence which history has not recorded, and which tradition has but imperfectly handed down. This town which, in covenanting times, was famous as the occasional haunt of our Scottish worthies, and especially for the *Declaration* which the followers of Cameron published at its cross, stands in an interesting part of the country. The scenery in its immediate vicinity wears, in some places, a magnificent aspect, and in others is unrivalled for its pastoral beauty and sweetness. The silvery streams of the Mennock and the Crawick present each a scene of grandeur which can scarcely be equalled and which have been deemed worthy of a panoramic exhibition in the first cities of the nation. The salubrity of its climate, owing to the purity and freshness of the air which streams down from the lofty and dry mountains by which the town is surrounded, is tested by the great age to which many of the inhabitants live, and by the absence of those epidemical diseases which prevail in other parts of the country. Nor is this burgh without its monuments of antiquity. It is itself one of the oldest towns in the south of Scotland. It is, as its name imports, of Celtic origin, but of a date too remote to be ascertained. Its castle, which, under the corroding hand of time, is fast crumbling to ruins, stands on a low embankment which once overlooked the classic stream of the Nith before the river assumed its present bed, and was in the days of our Scottish patriots, Wallace and Bruce, the scene of bloody conflicts; and its British encampment, so ancient that even tradition itself has forgotten it, is situated on a lovely green eminence to the north-west, commanding a full view of the beautiful basin to which Sanquhar gives the name. The old parish church, which a few years ago was demolished to make room for the handsome structure which now occupies its place, was coeval with the high church of Glasgow, and contained some of the hallowed relics of the olden time, such as the altar of the *haly bluid*, to see which, and to drink of consecrated waters of the limpid well of the far-famed Saint Bride, many a devout pilgrim came even from distant parts.

It has often been remarked, that the inhabitants of the district, for a few miles around Sanquhar, are much superior to their neighbours in point of intelligence and general propriety of conduct. This was especially noticed by Sir Walter Scott; and the circumstance may be so far attributed to those sources of information to which they have an easy access, the locality being furnished with no fewer than six libraries, and one of these comprehending nearly two thousand volumes.

This small town has been favoured with a sound gospel ministry since the Revolution, and prior to that era it was equally favoured. And as it was always in those places where the gospel was purely preached that the greatest host of witnesses for the truth arose, consequently those who drove the car of persecution over the breadth and length of a bleeding land had most to do in such localities. The solitudes in the upper parts of Nithsdale were the places of refuge to those who, on account of their faithful adherence to the testimony which they held, were driven from the bosom of their families to seek a home in the desert; and the imagination can scarcely conceive of solitudes more dreary and sterile than those which lie on the north-west borders of the parish of Sanquhar. From the top of any of the lofty heights in the vicinity of this wilderness, nothing can be discovered but rugged mountains of brown heath, and vast wastes of dark moorland, stretching onward for miles in the distance, with here and there the blue smoke curling from the chimneys of the lone huts of the shepherds. It was in the very heart of these solitudes, and in their most retired and unknown retreats, that the worthy men of another age betook themselves for shelter, braving the fierce blasts of the desert that they might escape the still fiercer storms of a relentless persecution. And many a stirring incident and perilous adventure, unknown to the historic page, are told of the witnessing remnant, before the shepherd's blazing hearth during the long winter evenings, by the inhabitants of the wilderness, many of whom are themselves descendants of the men whose memory they so warmly cherish, and the incidents of whose lives they so feelingly narrate. In traversing on a fine summer day, with an intelligent shepherd, the wilds which were once the asylum of men who deserved a better home, it is thrilling to listen to the anecdotes of varied interest which the features of the desert recall to the mind of your companion. There is the identical spot where the venerable Cargill held a conventicle, yonder the place where Cameron uttered the denunciations of divine vengeance against a gospel-proof generation; yonder the solitary shieling in which a company of God's hidden ones were surprised and captured by a brutal soldiery; and yonder the hill where the pious Peden was screened by a seasonable mist from the view of his blood-thirsty pursuers. In this way, almost every hill and streamlet and moss and cottage has its incident, and is endeared by hallowed associations. I shall narrate a few of those anecdotes, relative to the persecuting period, which are still in circulation among the people of the moorlands. They possess considerable interest, and are worthy of preservation for the sake of the men to whom they refer.

There was a worthy man of the name of Howatson, who, on account of his well-known attachment to covenanting principles, was obliged to keep himself in perpetual concealment among the more remote and unfrequented glens and mountains. His house was occasionally searched by the dragoons, sometimes by day and at other times by night, for the purpose of surprising him at some unwary hour in the bosom of his family. It happened on one occasion that Howatson ventured to spend the night under his own roof at a time when he did not expect a surprisal from his enemies; for it was generally when the snow lay on the ground, or when the solitudes were visited with a severe storm, that the good men who dwelt in the dens and caves of the wilderness durst enter their homes without risk. Under the cloud of night he stole into his lonely hut without being seen by a human eye. He received, as was to be expected, the cordial greeting of his household; a meal was instantly prepared, his affectionate wife changed his dripping clothes, and his shivering frame was warmed and enlivened by a huge fire of peats, the towering flame of which ascended far up the chimney. It was a happy occasion, and the glad family continued to converse on matters of deep and thoughtful interest till a late hour. At length all retired to rest, and it was not long before the husband and the father, worn out with hunger and fatigue and watchfulness, sunk into a profound sleep. But while this pious household were slumbering in fancied security from the intrusion of their enemies, those very enemies were at the door. They had set out in quest of their victim; having by some means been informed of his hiding-place; and not finding him there as they anticipated, they hoped to capture him in his own house. Accordingly, having reached the solitary dwelling at the dead of night, they stationed six of their number before the door, while four of them entered the house, having softly lifted the latch, the door, by an unaccountable oversight, having been left unlocked. At this juncture the wife of Howatson awoke, and, to her amazement, saw four men standing before the fire, attempting to light a candle; and rightly judging who the intruders were, she, without uttering a word, grasped her husband firmly by the arm. He instantly started up and saw the men, and, observing that their backs were towards him, he slipt gently from his bed on the clay floor, and stole softly to the door. It was guarded by the dragoons. He hesitated for a moment, and then darted like an arrow through the midst of them. The waving of his snow-white shirt, like a sheet of lightning, terrified the horses, and threw the party into confusion, and, though they fired several times, he escaped unscathed. He fled with the utmost speed to the house of a friend, where he obtained a lodging for the remainder of the night; and next day his clothing was conveyed to him by his wife, who could not but observe the hand of a special providence stretched out for the protection of her husband.

On another occasion, however, this same individual was not quite so fortunate, though he eventually escaped with his life. His enemies, being constantly in search of him, at length got hold of him, and the laird of Drumlanrig, the leader of the persecuting party in that district, brought him to his castle and confined him in a dungeon called "the pit of Drumlanrig." This prison-house was covered above with strong boards secured with massive bars of iron, so that escape was rendered impossible. In this place was Howatson incarcerated, not knowing the fate that might be awaiting him, whether he should be hanged aloft on the gallows tree before the castle gate, or shot by the dragoons on the lawn, or, worst of all, be left to perish with hunger in the pit. There lived in the neighbourhood a half-witted man of the name of Hastie, a person of very great bodily strength, and who frequently performed feats that were incredible. To this person the wife of Howatson offered a sum of money to attempt the rescue of her husband. His bodily prowess and his partial insanity amply qualified him for the undertaking, for by the one he could accomplish the work, and by the other he would be screened from punishment if caught in the attempt. Hastie agreed to the proposal, and, under the cloud of night, succeeded in removing the covering of the pit, and in effecting the release of the prisoner. Howatson, at length, wearied out by a ceaseless persecution, retired with a fellow-sufferer, of the name of Harkness, to Ireland, where he lived in concealment till the Revolution, when he returned to his native land and died in peace.

Another anecdote is told of a pious man named Hair, who lived in a secluded place called Burncrooks, near Kirkland, in the parish of Kirkconnel, a few miles to the west of Sanquhar. This inoffensive man was seized by his persecutors and doomed to die. The cruel and brutal conduct of the dragoons was peculiarly displayed in the treatment of this godly person. They rallied him on the subject of his death, and told him that they intended to kill him in a way that would afford them some merriment; that as his name was Hair, they wished to enjoy something of the same sport in putting an end to his life that they used to enjoy in killing the cowering and timid animal that bore a similar name. Instead, therefore, of shooting him before his own door, they placed him on horseback behind a dragoon, and carried him to the top of a neighbouring hill, that in the most conspicuous and insulting manner they might deprive him of his life. The spot where the cavalcade halted happened to be on the very brink of one of the most romantic glens in the west of Scotland. Glen Aylmer forms an immense cleft between two high mountains, and opens obliquely on the meridian sun. The descent on either side for several hundred feet is very steep, and in some places is almost perpendicular. The whole valley is clothed with rich verdure, and through its centre flows a gentle stream of many crooks and windings, appearing from the summit of the declivity like a silver thread stretching along the deep bottom of the glen. The breadth of this sweet vale is, generally speaking, not more perhaps than a hundred yards; and the whole scene strongly reminds one of the beautiful vale of Tempe, so graphically described by Ælian. And though there are here no altars smoking with incense, no thickets overshadowing the path by the side of the stream, to screen the weary traveller from the noon-day sun, no convivial parties regaling themselves in its groves, no musical birds warbling among the leafy branches of the ivy-mantled trees, as in the celebrated defile between Ossa and Olympus; yet, Glen Aylmer is a scene which, for simplicity and majesty, cannot easily be rivalled, and he who has seen it once will not grudge to look on it again.

The party of dragoons, then, having reached the spot where they intended to shoot their captive had made a halt for the purpose of dismounting, and the soldier behind whom our worthy was seated, proceeded to unbuckle the belt which, for greater security, we may suppose, bound the prisoner to his person; when Hair, finding himself disengaged, slid from the horse behind, and, light ing on the very edge of the steep declivity, glided with great swiftness down the grassy turf, and tumbling over and over, at last regained his feet and ran at his utmost speed till he reached the bottom. The soldiers looked with amazement, but durst not follow; they fired thick but missed him, and were left to gnaw their tongues in painful disappointment. What became of this good man tradition does not say; but on this occasion at least, he had reason to set up his stone of remembrance, and to say, "Hitherto hath the Lord helped me."

I shall here add another short anecdote of a young man of the name of William Adams, who lived in Wellwood, and who, on account of his piety and nonconforming principles, became an object of hostility to the persons who in those times sought every opportunity to harass and persecute the people of God. William, who was about to be married to an excellent and amiable young woman in the neighbourhood, had appointed a meeting with her in the moors. On the day specified he was first at the *trysting* place; and, in order to pass the time till his friend should arrive in the most profitable way, he opened his Bible and read the word of God. He had not long continued at this employment till his eye caught a party of dragoons close upon him; he started to his feet; the enemy rode up to him, and in an instant he was shot dead on the spot. The young woman, who was now advancing at a quick pace along the heath, heard the loud and startling report of fire arms precisely in the direction in which she was going; she walked onward with a throbbing heart and with a faltering step; she feared lest her beloved William had fallen by the savage hand of the foe; her worst suspicions seemed to be justified, when she saw several horsemen coming over the rising ground, apparently from the very place where she expected to meet with her lover. She met them just as she was passing along a narrow foot-bridge thrown by the shepherds for their own convenience over the mossy streamlet; and as they were crossing the brook close by the side of the bridge, one of the dragoons drew his sword, and jocularly struck her with its broad-side, under the pretence of pushing her into the water. Her spirit was embittered, and her courage was roused; and, wrapping her apron closely round her hand, she seized the sword by the blade, wrenched it from the grasp of the warrior, snapped it in two over her knee, and flung the pieces into the stream. With eager impatience she hastened to the meeting place. All her fears were realized: her William was lying stiff on the ground, and his blood had stained the heather bloom with a deeper dye.

It is worthy of remark that the annals of the persecuting period do not record the sufferings of almost any one belonging to the *parish* of Sanquhar, notwithstanding the many good men that must have lived in it at that time. Their exemption from persecution has been supposed to result in a great measure from the leniency of the curate, who was a good-natured, easy sort of man. Tradition says that, instead of seeking occasion against those of his parishioners who refused to submit to his ministry, he publicly announced that, if on a given day they would assemble within the church-yard, though they did not enter the church, he would give a favourable report of the whole parish, and screen the nonconformists from the vengeance of their persecutors. It would seem that this request was, to a certain extent at least, complied with. There is an anecdote current among the people of this neighbourhood, which displays in some measure, the humane disposition of the incumbent. Two of the covenanting brethren from the wilds of Carsfairn, in full flight before the dragoons, dashed into the river Nith and reached the opposite bank a few yards below the manse. It happened that a number of individuals, among whom was the curate, were playing at quoits on the green. "Where shall we run?" cried the two men. "Doff your coats," said the curate, "and play a game with me." They did so. The dragoons immediately followed; they passed the curate and rode on in pursuit, and the men, through his generous interference, escaped.

There is on the east bank of the river Crawick, near the town, and not far from the place where Sir William Douglas, many a century ago, concealed his men on the evening prior to the memorable day when he took the castle of Sanquhar from General Beauford, who commanded the English troops who occupied its fastness, an old ruined cavern said to be the frequent resort of the intercommuned wanderers. This place had two entrances, so that when they were assailed at the one, they escaped at the other. In the immediate neighbourhood of this retreat are the graves of two worthies, whose names are unknown, and who probably died of disease occasioned by the hardships to which they were exposed. We ought to cherish the memory of the men who, for the sake of truth, "jeoparded their lives on the high places of the field," and who, if they did not plant the tree of liberty, at least watered it with their blood.

CHAPTER II.

Peden in Glendyne—Woman at Inglestone—Craigdarroch.

About the commencement of the persecution in Scotland, nearly "three hundred and fifty ministers were ejected from their churches, in the severity of winter, and driven with their families, to seek shelter among the peasants. These ministers were forbidden to preach even in the fields, or to approach within twenty miles of their former charges; and all the people, as well as their pastors, who were not prepared to abjure their dearest rights, and submit to the most galling and iniquitous civil and religious despotism, were denounced as traitors." None were allowed in any way to assist them, or even to supply them with food, or to shelter them in their houses; and those whose humanity or Christian principles inclined them to show kindness to those friendless followers of Christ, exposed their property and their persons to the rapacity and cruelty of a wicked and injurious policy. The apostle's description of the destitute condition of the ancient people of God, in persecuting times, is literally true of our forefathers: "They wandered in deserts and in mountains, and in dens and in caves of the earth." But "they took joyfully the spoiling of their goods, knowing that in heaven they had a better and an enduring substance." Often in the moorland solitudes, concealed from the vigilant eye of their persecutors, did these devoted servants of the Redeemer open the wells of salvation for the refreshment of God's weary heritage, who, thirsting for the water of life, resorted to them in crowds; and many a blessed outpouring of the gracious Spirit of God was experienced by them, when, in the hallowed retreat of the wilderness, they congregated at the risk of all that was dear to them on earth to worship the God of their fathers—the enemies of God and his holy evangel not permitting them to assemble in temples made with hands. The Saviour, however, bore testimony to the word of his own grace, and to the worthiness of that cause for which his people were suffering, in filling the hearts of his followers with comfort, and in crowning the ministrations of his servants with success.

The desolation and distress of many a family, after the standard of the gospel was reared in the fields, were unutterable. The tender-hearted wife knew not how it fared with her husband traversing the waste, or lodged in the cold damp cave; and many a disconsolate hour did she spend in weeping over her helpless children, who had apparently nothing before them but starvation. The affectionate husband, far from his dearly cherished home, was full of the bitter remembrance of his beloved family, and picturing to himself their many wants which he could not now relieve, and their many sorrows which he could not soothe, and the many insults from which he could not defend them. But, notwithstanding all this, they had peace; for God was with them. And though their hearts sometimes misgave them, yet, through the grace of him with whose cause they were identified, their faith recovered its proper tone, and their despondency vanished.

One of the most renowned of those worthies who persisted in preaching the gospel in the wilds of his native land, at the constant hazard of his life, was the venerable Peden, whose history is fa miliar in almost every cottage in Scotland. Every incident of any importance in the life of this gooa man has already been collected, so that scarcely any thing new can now be added. Still there is to be found a stray anecdote of him here and there in the remote parts of the country, and which, for his sake, may be deemed worthy of record, Few persons possessed a more saintly character than did this man of God. He was full of faith and of the Holy Ghost. Entirely devoted to his Master's service, he counted not his own life dear unto him, that he might maintain the cause of truth in the face of the abounding iniquity of a degenerate age. His solitary wanderings, his destitutions, his painful perseverance in preaching the gospel, the peril in which he lived, his prayerful spirit, and the homeliness of his manners, greatly endeared him to the people among whom he sojourned. He had no home, and therefore he spent much of his time in the fields. The caves by the mountain stream, the dense hazel wood in the deep glens, the feathery brackens on the hill, the green corn when it was tall enough to screen him from observation, afforded him by turns, when necessary, a retreat from his pursuers, and a place for communing with his God.

Among the many hiding-places to which this man, of whom the world was not worthy, occasionally retreated, was the solitude of Glendyne, about three miles to the east of Sanquhar. A more entire seclusion than this is rarely to be found. Glendyne stretches eastward, winding among the hills for nearly three miles. The width of the glen at the bottom is in many places little more than five or six times the breadth of the brawling torrent that rushes through it. Dark precipitous mountains, frowning on either side, rise from the level of the valley to an immense height. On the eastern extremity of the glen a cluster of hills gather to a point, and form an eminence of great altitude, from which a noble prospect of a vast extent of country is obtained. Near the lower end of this defile, which in ancient times was thickly covered with wood, and where it terminates its sinuous course with one majestic sweep, reaching forward to the bleak moorlands beneath, our revered worthy had selected for himself a place of refuge. This spot, deeply concealed by the dark mantling of the forest, was known only to a few who made the cause of these sufferers their own. It happened, on one occasion, that this honoured servant of Christ, having emerged from his covert, stood by the margin of the forest, on the beautiful slope of the mountain above. It was the balmy month of May, and nature had just put on her loveliest attire. The forest was vocal with the sweetest music. The blackbird and the thrush were piping their richest notes on the "green wood tree;" the gentle cooing of the wood-dove issued with a delicious softness from the grove; and the joyous lark, high in the air, was pouring a flood of melody down upon the wilderness. The wild bees were humming among the honeyed blossoms of the hawthorn; the scented wind, breathing over the fragrant heath, was playing with the rustling foliage; the brook was murmuring in the ravine below; the lambkins were gambolling on the verdant lea, and the sheep were grazing quietly by their side, while on the distant hill the shepherd was seen, wrapped in his plaid, with his sportive dog at his foot, slowly winding his way up the steep ascent. The good man's heart beat high with rapture—his delighted eye roamed over the charming variety of hill and dale—he contemplated the glorious sun, and all the splendid scenery of the sky—he felt as if he were standing on holy ground, in the midst of the great temple of nature—he experienced an unusual elevation of mind, and all the freshness and buoyancy of youth seemed once more to take possession of his aged frame. Full of devout sentiment he uncovered his head, the silvery hairs of which were streaming on his shoulders, and, lifting up his hands, he 'praised, and honoured, and extolled the King of heaven, all whose works are truth, and whose ways are judgment.' He had fixed his eye on a cottage far off in the waste, in which lived a godly man, with whom he had frequent intercourse; and there being nothing within view calculated to excite alarm, he resolved to pay his friend a visit. With his staff in his hand, he wended his way to the low grounds to gain the track which led to the house. He reached it in safety, was hospitably entertained by the kind landlord, and spent the time with the household, in pious conversation and prayer, till sunset. Not daring to remain all night, he left them to return to his dreary cave. As he was trudging along the soft foot-path, and suspecting no harm, all at once several moss-troopers appeared coming over the bent, and advancing directly upon him. He fled across the moor, and when about to pass the torrent that issues from Glendyne, he accidentally perceived a cavity underneath its bank, that had been scooped out by the running stream, into which he instinctively crept, and stretching himself at full length, lay hidden beneath the grassy coverlet, waiting the result. In a short time the dragoons came up, and having followed close in his track, reached the brook at the very spot where he was ensconced. As the heavy horses came thundering over the smooth turf, on the edge of the rivulet, the foot of one of them sank quite through the hollow covering under which the object of their pursuit lay. The hoof of the animal grazed his head, and pressed his bonnet deep into the soft clay at his pillow, and left him entirely uninjured. His persecutors having no suspicion that the poor fugitive was so near them, crossed the stream with all speed, and bounded away in quest of him whom God had thus hidden as in his pavilion, and in the secret of his tabernacle. A man like Peden, who read the hand of God in every thing, could not fail to see and to acknowledge that Divine goodness, which was so eminently displayed in this instance; and we may easily conceive with what feelings he would return to his retreat in the wood, and with what cordiality he would send up the voice of thanksgiving and praise to the God of his life.

It is recorded in the Scots Worthies, that he was favoured with a memorable deliverance from the enemy, who were pursuing him and a small company with him, somewhere in Galloway, after he came out of Ireland. When their hope of escape was almost cut off, he knelt down among the heather and prayed, "Twine them about the hill, Lord, and cast the lap of thy cloak over old Sandy and these poor things, and we will keep it in remembrance and tell it to the commendation of thy goodness, pity, and compassion, what thou didst for us at such a time." Thus he prayed, and his supplication was recorded in heaven; for he had no sooner risen from his knees than dense volumes of snow-white m st came rolling down from the summit of the mountains, and shrouded them from the sight of their pursuers, who, like the men of Sodom, when they were smitten with blindness, could not grope their way after them. Auchengrouch hill, in the vicinity of Glendyne, was the scene of a similar incident. Truly they are a blessed people whose God is the Lord, for in the time of their calamity he is their help and their shield, and "they need not be afraid of ten thousands of people who have set themselves against them round about, for salvation belongeth unto the Lord, and his blessing is upon his people."

There is a story told of a woman who resided at a place called Ingleston, in the parish of Glencairn, about eighteen miles to the south of Sanquhar, whose remarkable preservation in the very presence of her enemies, who were eagerly seeking her life, is no less illustrative of the watchful providence of God than the anecdote which has now been related, and which confirms the truth of the adage, that "every man is immortal till his day come." This woman, whose name is not mentioned, was a "mother in Israel." Her truly religious character, and her refusal to attend the ministry of the Curate, did not escape the notice of the dominant party, who, in those times of oppression, sought "to wear out the saints of the most High." The name of the master whom she served was too conspicuously imprinted on her forehead to admit of concealment. A party of horsemen were one day despatched to the place of her residence in search of her. They were near the house before they were observed, and the worthy woman, guessing their errand, ran for refuge to the barn, in which a female servant wás busily employed at her work. "The dragoons, the dragoons," cried the fugitive, "where shall I hide?" "Run to that corner," said the servant, "and I will cover you with the straw." The soldiers rushed into the barn, expecting instantly to seize their prey; and seeing nobody but the servant, who refused to give them any satisfactory information, in their rage and disappointment, they began to kick among the straw; and drawing their long swords they thrust them at full length, with all their force, through the heaps with which the barn floor was covered, stabbing vengefully in every corner where they thought there was any likelihood of concealment. The nook, however, into which the object of their search had crept had either been missed by them, or their swords did not hit on the precise spot where she lay; for, notwithstanding the closeness of the search, she remained undiscovered and unscathed. In this astonishing manner, then, did the Lord preserve another of his saints who trusted in him, throwing over her the shield of his effectual protection in circumstances in which, to human view, there was no probability of escape.

But the rage of persecuting malignity was not confined in its object merely to the humbler orders of the land, who had neither power nor influence to protect them: it vented itself with equal violence on those who occupied a higher and more commanding station in society—like the desolating storm which descends indiscriminately on the lofty mountains and on the lowly valleys. The attachment of the house of Craigdarroch in Glencairn, to the principles of the covenanters, is well known; and many an outcast, in the days of our forefathers, took refuge under its sheltering wings. The master of Craigdarroch was, therefore, a marked man, and his enemies were determined to show him no favour. It happened on a fine summer morning, when, after a heavy rain which fell during the preceding night, the rivers and burns were greatly swollen, that the laird, as he was termed, was under the necessity of travelling a short distance from home. Orders had been issued to a party of dragoons to watch his movements, and to embrace the first opportunity of seizing his person. As he was ambling slowly along on a fine spirited horse, he was all at once confronted with a company of troopers. The place where they met was at the opening of a stone dyke, through which the road passed. The commander of the party, who seemed to know the laird, cried, " Guard the gap." " I'll guard the gap," replied the laird, who at the same time turning the head of his swift and powerful steed, galloped off at his utmost speed. The horsemen pursued, and Craigdarroch seeing that there was but little hope of escape, directed his course to the river Cairn, which at the time was in full flood, and dashed into its foaming torrent, choosing rather to risk his life in the tumultuous waters than be captured by a savage soldiery. He reached the opposite bank, upon which the noble animal landed him with a bound. By the sudden spring two of the nine girths by which his saddle is said to have been secured, were ruptured. The dragoons having noticed the circumstance, bawled out that now he was their prisoner. " Not yet," vociferated our hero, now on the safe side of the stream, " for though two of the bands be broken, there yet remain seven stout and firm ; and now I dare you to the pursuit; throw yourselves into that roaring tide and follow me." This, however, was a challenge which none of them were inclined to accept, for the conviction that they are engaged in a bad cause generally makes men cowards. In this way this worthy man, under the conduct of a gracious providence, was rescued from the ruthless hands of those who would have shown him no mercy. It is reported that the identical saddle on which the honoured ancestor of the house of Craigdarroch sat on this occasion, is still preserved by the family.

It was in Craigdarroch house where John Stevenson, the Ayreshire covenanter, lodged in secrecy in some of the hottest days of persecution. His wife, who was nurse to Craigdarroch's child, was greatly esteemed by the lady of the mansion, and for her sake the husband was admitted under hiding, into a private apartment of the house. His abode there was known to none, not even to the laird himself; but the household was blessed for his sake, for his prayers were heard for them in the day of their distress. The Lord never allows any to be losers for his people's sake; even "a cup of cold water given to a disciple, in the name of a disciple, shall not lose its reward." And it is worthy of remark, that those who, in the time of the church's tribulation, aided the suffering followers of Christ in any way, and especially those who did so, at the risk of losing their worldly property or their life, were afterwards prosperous in temporal things; for our Lord takes a special notice of every act of kindness done to his people for his sake: "Inasmuch as ye did it unto the least of these my brethren, ye did it unto me."

The brief history of John Stevenson, written by himself, is well worthy of a perusal. It breathes throughout a spirit of genuine piety and zeal and confidence in God. It records his religious experiences—the remarkable providences that befel him—the particular passages of Scripture that afforded him the subject of sweet meditation and comfort—and his last and best advice to his children. In the veritable history of such a man we have a practical commentary on the promises and providence of God, calculated to put infidelity to the blush, and to reprove the unbelief of the Lord's own people.

CHAPTER III.

Sanquhar Declaration—Conventicle in Blagannach Moss.

The Sanquhar *Declaration* was published by the followers of Cameron, on the 22d of June, 1680, exactly one year after the battle of Bothwell, and a month prior to his own death at Aird Moss. This declaration deserves notice, both on account of the prominence given to it at the time by the persecuted remnant, and also because it was assumed, on the part of the malignants, as a ground of criminal prosecution against those who acknowledged its propriety. "Do you own the Sanquhar declaration?" was a query, to which an answer in the affirmative subjected the individual to whatever punishment the caprice of the judges in the council, or the military in the field, might see proper to inflict. It was regarded as a manifesto of a highly treasonable nature, for it in plain terms disowned Charles as the lawful king of these realms; and thus, coming so soon after the affair of Bothwell bridge, it was the means of stimulating, to a very high pitch, the persecuting fury of the times. The attention of the ruling faction was now more especially directed to that part of the country where this declaration was made public; and a hireling soldiery was found the ready instrument of a merciless execution. As this declaration, on account of which so many worthy people of the land were brought into trouble, is now probably little known, we shall here give a reprint of it: it is brief, and will not detain the reader long.

"The Declaration and Testimony of the True Presbyterian, Anti-prelatic, Anti-erastian, persecuted party in Scotland. Published at Sanquhar, June 22, 1680.

"It is not amongst the smallest of the Lord's mercies to this poor land, that there have been always some who have given their testimony against every cause of defection, that many are guilty of, which is a token for good that he doth not as yet intend to cast us off altogether, but that he will leave a remnant in whom he will be glorious, if they, through his grace, keep themselves clean still, and walk in his way and method as it has been walked in, and owned by him in our predecessors of truly worthy memory; in their carrying on of our noble work of reformation, in the several steps thereof from Popery, Prelacy, and likewise Erastian supremacy—so much usurped by him, who, it is true, so far as we know, is descended from the race of our kings; yet he hath so far debased from what he ought to have been, by his perjury and usurpation in church matters, and tyranny in matters civil, as is known by the whole land, that we have just reason to account it one of the Lord's great controversies against us that we have not disowned him, and the men of his practices, whether inferior magistrates or any other as enemies to our Lord and his crown, and the true Protestant and Presbyterian interests in their lands, our Lord's espoused bride and church. Therefore, although we be for government and governors, such as the word of God and our covenant allows, yet we, for ourselves, and all that will adhere to us as the representative of the true Presbyterian kirk and covenanted nation of Scotland, considering the great hazard of lying under such a sin any longer, do by these presents disown Charles Stuart that has been reigning, or rather tyrannizing, as we may say, on the throne of Britain these years bygone, as having any right, title to, or interest in, the said Crown of Scotland for government, as forfeited several years since, by his perjury and breach of covenant both to God and his kirk, and usurpation of his crown and royal prerogatives therein, and many other breaches in matters ecclesiastic, and by his tyranny and breach of the very *leges regnandi* in matters civil. For which reason, we declare, that several years since he should have been denuded of being king, ruler, or magistrate, or of having any power to act or to be obeyed as such. As also we being under the standard of our Lord Jesus Christ, Captain of Salvation, do declare a war with such a tyrant and usurper, and all the men of his practices, as enemies to our Lord Jesus Christ and his cause and covenants; and against all such as have strengthened him, sided with, or anywise acknowledged him in his tyranny, civil or ecclesiastic—yea, against all such as shall strengthen, side with, or anywise acknowledge any other in like usurpation and tyranny—far more against such as would betray or deliver up our free reformed mother kirk unto the bondage of antichrist, the Pope of Rome. And by this we homologate that testimony given at Rutherglen the 29th of May, 1679, and all the faithful testimonies of those who have gone before, as also of those who have suffered of late. And we do disclaim that declaration published at Hamilton, June 1679, chiefly because it takes in the king's interest which we are several years since loosed from, because of the aforesaid reasons and others which may after this, if the Lord will, be published. As also we disown, and by this resent the reception of the Duke of York, that professed Papist, as repugnant to our principles and vows to the most high God, and as that which is the great, though not alone, just reproach of our kirk and nation. We also, by this protest against his succeeding to the crown, and whatever has been done, or any are essaying to do in this land, given to the Lord, in prejudice to our work of reformation. And to conclude, we hope after this none will blame us for, or offend at, our rewarding those that are against us as they have done to us, as the Lord gives opportunity. This is not to exclude any that have declined, if they be willing to give satisfaction according to the degree of their offence."

Such, then, is the famous declaration, which made so much noise at the time of its publication, and to which so much importance was attached by its adherents. This, however, is not the only declaration which was published at the cross of Sanquhar. There were five besides this; one by Mr. Renwick about three years before the Revolution, and four after it, by the parties who were not satisfied with the existing state of things. Of the four declarations which were published at Sanquhar after the Revolution, the first was August 10, 1692

—the second, November 6, 1695—the third, May 21, 1703—and the fourth, 1707. This ancient burgh seems to have been fruitful in declarations. It is the central point of a wide district, which at that time was the favourite resort of many of the sufferers, and a place which was of easy access from every quarter.

The following anecdotes, however, are connected, not with the first of these declarations, but with the second, published by Renwick after the death of Charles II., and the proclamation of the Duke of York as king, in 1685. "Mr. Renwick," says his biographer, "could not let go this opportunity of witnessing against the usurpation by a Papist of the government of the nation, and his design of overthrowing the covenanted work of reformation, and introducing Popery. Accordingly, he and about two hundred men went to Sanquhar, May 28, 1685, and published the declaration, afterwards called the Sanquhar Declaration."

The year 1685 was, perhaps, with the exception of the year in which the Highland host was let loose in the west, the darkest in the annals of the persecuting period. It is termed by Wodrow, "a black year." During this year the blood of the saints was made to run like water on the ground; and many a loud cry did it send up to that holy heaven, which witnessed the sufferings of those devoted ones who loved not their lives unto the death. "How long, O Lord, holy and true, dost thou not judge and avenge our blood on them that dwell on the earth? And white robes were given unto every one of them; and it was said unto them that they should rest yet for a little season, until their fellow-servants also, and their brethren that should be killed as they were, should be fulfilled.' Satan, knowing that his time was but short, seemed to rage with uncommon fury, and vigorously strove "to wear out the saints of the Most High."

A short time after the accession of James, Mr. Renwick held a conventicle in the moor of Evandale. A great company assembled from all quarters to hear the word of truth preached by this youthful and zealous servant of Christ, who, almost single-handed, maintained the standard of the gospel in the fields. After the day's work was concluded, a meeting was held on the spot, for the purpose of deliberating on what, in the present posture of affairs, was best to be done. After much consultation, it was agreed that a full declaration of their principles should be published at the cross of Sanquhar on an early day. They were convinced that no redress of their grievances was to be obtained: they saw that they could not rectify matters for themselves, and that the only thing left for them to do was to testify publicly and strongly against the evil complained of. It was stated by some present that Mr. Shiels had lately returned from Ireland, and was under hiding in the west: it was therefore agreed that before any thing definitive was done, another meeting should be convened in a glen a few miles to the north-west of Sanquhar, and that Mr. Renwick and Mr. Shiels together should concert measures respecting the proposed declaration. Having, therefore, come to this determination, the assembly dispersed, every one being enjoined to observe the strictest secrecy. It was not an easy matter, however, to secure the secrecy necessary in such cases; for it was not possible to hold any meeting, even in the remotest solitudes, without the intrusion of spies and informers, who appeared among them as wolves in sheep's clothing, and who, by goodly words and fair speeches, insinuated themselves into the good graces of the simple-minded people who, practising no deceit themselves, were not so ready to suspect others. The appointed day of meeting at length arrived. Mr. Renwick, who at this time lodged in a place called Cumberhead, where he was kindly entertained for his Master's sake, had a journey of about twenty miles to accomplish. He was accompanied by a few faithful friends, one of whom, named Laing, a steady adherent of the cause, lived in Blagannach, not far from the place of the supposed meeting. Blagannach is situated in the very heart of the mountains, about half-way between Sanquhar and Muirkirk, and near Hyndbottom, the lonely scene of a great conventicle held on one occasion by Cameron. The locality affords a specimen of one of the most perfect solitudes in the south Highlands, and, in former times, when the glens were not opened by roads nor cleared of their woods, would not be easily accessible. The Laings of Blagannach are a very ancient family, their race having now been resident in that place for nearly four hundred years. The road between Cumberhead and the place where the conventicle was to be held, was very rough and mountainous, and not easily travelled on horseback. Mr. Renwick and his company, therefore, set out on foot the evening before. The night-season was adopted for the purpose of concealment; and after many a weary and toilsome step, they reached the spot in the early morning. As they came along, groups of people were seen gathering in from all parts to the secluded glen. The numbers that were assembling showed the deep interest which the populace generally took in the matter. When a goodly number of the people had congregated, and were silently waiting till the services should commence, a man on horseback was descried in the distance, advancing with all the speed that the ruggedness of the ground would permit. The deep murmuring of voices was heard throughout the congregation, like the low muttering of remote thunder. It was obvious to every one that the horseman was the bearer of important tidings; this was indicated by his hurried and impatient movements. Every heart throbbed with solicitude, and the anxiety of the moment was intense. At length the approach of the messenger put an end to suspense. "Ye are betrayed, my friends!" vociferated he, when he was within cry of the company: "Ye are betrayed, and the enemy is at hand." This was indeed the case: a traitor had found his way into the camp at the former meeting, and he lost no time in communicating the designs of the party to the enemy. This informer was a man of the name of Sandilands from Crawford-John, who had been seen in company with the commander of the dragoons on the evening preceding. This infamous character was in the pay of the enemy; and he exerted himself in every way to gain the good opinion of his employers, and to retain his lucrative situation.

This information spread consternation throughout the meeting, and it was resolved instantly to abandon he spot, and to retire to a still more secluded place among the mountains; and the neighbourhood of Blagannach was fixed on as the place of retreat. The tent, under the awning of which Mr. Renwick was to address the multitude, was erected on the edge of an impassable morass, and was constructed of strong stakes driven deep into the moss, and covered with the plaids of the shepherds. Before the work of the day commenced, it was agreed that Mr. Renwick should exchange clothes with some individual present. The design of this, was, that, in case of the sudden appearance of the troopers, he might the more readily effect his escape. There was no small danger attending this experiment to the man who should assume Mr. Renwick's dress—as a person in clerical habiliments would, in these times, be easily distinguishable from the rest of the people. Laing, however, was ready to incur all the risk attending the project; and he generously offered to substitute himself in Mr. Renwick's stead. He was a stout and intrepid man, and fully prepared for a tough pursuit by the enemy, should they make their appearance. Mr. Renwick was forced to comply with the wishes of the company, and to attire himself for the present in a garb different from his own, but not an inappropriate one, for it was the garb of a shepherd. This was done with a most generous intention, for Mr. Renwick, possessing a constitution by no means robust, was much exhausted with the toil of the previous night's journey, and therefore incapacitated for much exertion in flight before his pursuers.

When all things were arranged, and the watches stationed at proper distances to give due warning in case of danger, this little church convened in the wilderness, engaged in the solemn worship of God. The words from which Mr. Renwick preached were, "He that toucheth you, toucheth the apple of his eye." This text, it would appear, was selected for the occasion; and it is expressive of the peculiarity of the Lord's care and sympathy in reference to his people, whose enemies are watching the opportunity of injuring them. The eye is a very delicate and sensitive organ, and there is no part of the body which we are ready to defend with a more instinctive promptitude. Hence he who harms his people touches Christ in the tenderest part, and inflicts an injury which he is prepared to resent. This subject, then, would be employed by the preacher for the purpose of strengthening the faith and the fortitude of the handful that had now met among the mountains to bear witness to the truth. There is something exceedingly soothing and encouraging in the thought that God exercises over us a special guardianship as his people, that the shield of his providential interference is interposed between us and our foes, and that the sympathies of Christ are ever awake in our behalf.

As the company were listening to the discourse, with minds deeply absorbed in the subject, the work was suddenly interrupted by the report that the dragoons were within a quarter of a mile of the spot. All was confusion, and the congregation was instantly scattered. The greater part fled to the moss, where the dragoons could not so easily follow them. Laing, arrayed in Mr. Renwick's clothes, took a different route; and rendered himself as conspicuous as possible, for the purpose of attracting the notice of the dragoons to himself, singly and alone, as the supposed individual after whom they were chiefly in quest. The stratagem succeeded; and the main body of the troopers turned in the direction in which he was fleeing, and this afforded the people and Mr. Renwick the opportunity of escaping. Laing, acting as a decoy, led the soldiers into the deepest and most inextricable parts of the morass. He knew every foot of it, and could wend his way with ease through its entire breadth and length. In these morasses there are generally narrow paths that are known only to the shepherds, who can pass and repass with perfect safety, where strangers might probably lose their lives. Laing, and the few men that were with him, endeavoured to preserve a certain distance from the pursuers—not to advance too far, lest they should give up the chase as hopeless, and turn on the others—and not to proceed too tardily, lest their enemies should get within shot of them. The troopers seemed to have no doubt that the person whom they were following was Mr. Renwick, both from his appearance, and from the assistance which they saw was occasionally lent him in stepping the deep moss hags. The individual about whom so much solicitude was manifested could be no other than the minister; and therefore they were determined to capture him, come of the rest what might. When the horsemen had advanced a certain way into the moss, the impossibility of advancing further became instantly apparent; and, therefore, it was agreed that two or three of the more robust of the party should dismount and pursue on foot. In a short time, however, it was found that this method was equally impracticable; for the tall, heavy men, with their unwieldy accoutrements, leaping and plunging in the moss, sunk to the waist, and could with difficulty extricate themselves. In this attempt one of their number broke his leg, and this incident put an end to their pursuit. They dragged their disabled companion to the firm ground, and conveyed him to Blagannach. The good wife of Blagannach was the only person who was within when the party arrived; the rest of the family, who were at the conventicle, not having yet returned. The soldiers behaved very rudely, and questioned her losely respecting her sons and her husband. The honest woman, however, seemed to pay very little regard to their inquiries, professing to be greatly distressed at the loss of a good milch cow that had that morning disappeared in the moss. After they had refreshed themselves with what provisions they found in the house, perceiving that they could elicit nothing satisfactory from the old matron, they departed, being themselves the only party who that day had sustained damage. They marched to Crawford-John, where they left their comrade with the fractured limb till he should recover. Tradition says that the soldier who met with the accident became an altered man; that during his confinement he began seriously to reflect on the course he had been pursuing; that the iniquity of his conduct became clearly apparent; that he was led to true repentance and faith in the Saviour; and that, after his recovery, he connected himself with the cause he had persecuted, and lived a zealous devoted Christian. It is exceedingly gratifying to meet with such an instance of a gracious change in an individual whose employment was to shed the blood of the saints. Such conversions, though not numerous, were nevertheless of occasional occurrence; the Lord manifesting his graciousness here and there as something noticeable, and as an encouragement to others of the same profession to turn to him, in the certain hope of likewise obtaining mercy The gospel extends the offer of salvation to sinners of every description: the greatest as well as the least sinner is welcome to come to him, who is able to save to the uttermost; for the blood of Christ cleanseth from all sin. Saul the persecutor found mercy; one "who made havoc of the church of God, entering into every house, and haling men and women, committed them to prison"—and the mercy that Saul obtained, others also may obtain. The forgiveness of great and notorious transgressors eminently illustrates the sovereignty and richness of Divine grace, and displays the infinite efficacy of the Christian atonement, and shows that there is no sin so great but God is ready to forgive it for the Redeemer's sake. "Though your sins be as scarlet, they shall be white as snow; and though they be red like crimson, they shall be as the wool." This poor man was the only individual of his party who met with anything like a serious accident in their attempt to disperse and kill the worshippers of God in the desert; and he was, perhaps, the only one of their entire number who was brought to the knowledge of the truth. Afflictions are often messengers of mercy, which the Lord sends to "bring back his banished;" and, though the fracture of the soldier's leg would doubtless be deemed by him as the greatest calamity that could befal him next to the loss of his life, yet God made it the precursor of his conversion. It sometimes happens that an occurrence which we regard at the time as a very great misfortune, turns out in the event to be a great blessing. We are short-sighted creatures; and are therefore ready to draw the most unfavourable conclusions from apparently disastrous incidents, which, nevertheless, embody the greatest good, and issue in our special benefit. "All these things are against me," exclaimed the venerable patriarch, when in truth the whole was secretly working out the temporal salvation of his household. To bring good out of evil is the prerogative of him who is "wonderful in counsel, and excellent in working."

Blagannach, when we consider its situation and the Christian character of its occupants, must have been a place of frequent resort in the times of ecclesiastical oppression. It is said that in this place Alexander Shiels wrote part of the "Hind Let Loose," a work which well deserves a perusal, even in these enlightened times of civil and religious liberty.

The congregation, having fled on the approach of the dragoons, pursued their way down the rivulet of the Spanack, or Spank, towards the river Crawick. The Crawick is a pastoral stream which rises on the borders of Lanarkshire in the Highlands, and wends its way in a south-westerly direction till it falls into the Nith, in the immediate vicinity of Sanquhar. The course of this stream exhibits a scene of surpassing beauty; its mountains, covered with deep verdure, present the appearance of a newly mown meadow, while some of the hills are so abrupt from the summit to the base that a person can scarcely walk with steadiness along the velvet slope. The hollow valley of the Crawick was, at the time to which these sketches refer, closely covered with wood, whose thickets afforded a secure retreat to the fugitives from Blagannach moss. Into this place of concealment it was in vain for the dragoons to penetrate, and therefore they retired, satisfied that they had at least scattered the conventicle, though they had captured none of the rebels.

The leaders of the dispersed multitude met on

the evening of the same day, in a sequestered glade in the dark forest of Crawick, to concer measures anew respecting the Declaration. It was agreed that, though they were disappointed in their object, they would by no means abandon the design, but that, on a future day, they would meet again to fulfil their purpose. The publication of their projected Declaration they considered as an important duty which they owed alike to God and to their country; and a work which, in the present emergency, they were imperiously called on to perform. They therefore appointed a day for a second convention; and, commending one another to the grace of God and to the care of his providence, they dispersed to their several homes, thanking the Lord for the special protection which had that day been vouchsafed to them.

After the noise which the affair at Blagannach made had ceased, those friendly to the covenanting interest convened from Lesmahago and the neighbouring parishes, for the purpose of proceeding to the inland burgh of Sanquhar to publish the Declaration agreed on. About two hundred individuals met accordingly, determined to brave every opposition in the performance of a duty so imperative. On the 28th of May, 1685, the inhabitants of Sanquhar were surprised at the appearance of so great a company, who, without any signal of their approach, had stationed themselves in the very heart of their town. The men had a warlike aspect, each prepared with weapons of defence in case of an onslaught. In these unsettled times, when rumours of battles and of bloodshed were constantly ringing in people's ears, it is not to be wondered at that the populace of this quiet and secluded town should have felt some degree of alarm at the unceremonious intrusion of so great a band of men. Their purpose, however, was soon divulged. They were not come to pillage the inhabitants, or to spill one drop of blood, but to testify publicly their adherence to the covenanted cause of reformation, in the only way which was left open for them to do. Having, therefore, read their Declaration aloud in the audience of the people, and then attached it to the cross as their avowed testimony against the evils of which they virtuously complained, they, in a peaceable and orderly manner, left the place with all convenient speed, lest the enemy, to whom information of their proceedings would instantly be transmitted, should pursue them. This second Declaration, which was published with much more pomp and circumstance than the first by Cameron's party, was equally offensive, if not more so, to the civil authorities; for as the one disowned Charles, the other abjured James as an obnoxious Papist to whom no allegiance was lawfully due.

With regard to the propriety of the various Declarations which were published in these times of oppression, different persons will doubtless entertain different opinions. But, we would ask, is not the Revolution settlement founded on the principles contained in these Declarations! And, in 1688, did not the whole nation do on a larger scale exactly what the Covenanters of Scotland did on a small scale? Dr. Burns, the pious and talented editor of Wodrow, in his excellent "Preliminary Dissertation" to that work, makes the following remark: "The conduct of the actors in the scenes of Rutherglen, at Sanquhar, and at Torwood, in disowning the king, and excommunicating him and his adherents, is indeed justly censurable as rash and unwarranted. But we beg to know wherein did the primary principles avowed and acted on, on those occasions differ from those principles, which, in the course of a very few years thereafter, roused the dormant spirit of the country, and chased the oppressor from the throne?" Let those, then, who glory in the Revolutionary settlement take care how they censure the principles of the honest Covenanters of the North.

CHAPTER IV.

Scar—James McMichael.

The farm-house of Dalzien is situated in the centre of the valley of the Scar, and is famous as the birthplace of Daniel McMichael, who suffered martyrdom, and of James McMichael his brother, the subject of the following sketch. The Scar is a pastoral stream, which runs parallel to the Nith on the south, opposite Sanquhar, and separated by an intervening ridge of lofty mountains. The valley is adorned with a considerable variety of scenery; the upper part is plain and uninteresting, but towards the lower extremity it is enchanting. The chief feature of its topography, however, is an enormous rock, called Glenquhargen crag, which, from the plain of the valley, rises probably to the height of about six hundred feet. The south of Scotland, perhaps, can boast of nothing of the same description of equal magnificence. The height of the naked rock, however, is much less at present than it must have been in former ages, for its base is now deeply buried in its own debris. It is one of those bold features of nature which inspires the beholder with the mingled feelings of delight and awe. This stupendous scene has its own legends connected with the covenanting times, but fraught with a superstition too gross to admit of recital. Dalzien stands at the head of a charming triangular opening of the valley, as green and level as a velvet lawn, and lined on the three sides with hills of a moderate elevation, while the pure stream of the Scar sweeps along its northern edge. The entire appearance of the scene, at first sight, strongly reminds one of some of those beautiful Waldensian valleys, in the secrecy of which the Church of God concealed herself for ages. Nor was the character of the inhabitants dissimilar; for even to a recent period, the locality was peopled with a race of eminent Christians, the fame of whose genuine worth was not confined to their own neighbourhood.

James McMichael was a man of a bold and hasty temper, and was easily roused to great energy in the defence of what in his conscience he believed to be the right cause. His temper, however, was frequently a source of uneasiness to his friends, as well as of terror to his enemies, and it required no small share of Divine grace to subdue it, and to keep it within proper bounds. His irascibility accounts for the impetuous and reprehensible manner in which he sometimes acted, and throws a considerable shade over his otherwise worthy character. The period in which tradition first brings him into notice is, when he was in the service of the Laird of Maxwellton, and when, on account of the discovery of his religious and political principles, he was obliged to flee for his life. He betook himself to the mountains, avowedly embraced the cause of the Covenanters, and resolved to share their fortunes. He assisted at the skirmish in Aird moss, where Richard Cameron and a number of his followers fell, defending themselves against the horsemen of Bruce of Earlshall. His patriotic feelings were easily kindled: and being informed by some of the refugees from Ayrshire, who came seeking a retreat among the dark mountains in the upper parts of Galloway, that the enemy were making strict search for Cameron and his followers, he forthwith resolved to join them. With this determination he left his hiding-place on the banks of the Ken, and set out to render what assistance he could to those with whom in their affliction he deeply sympathized. He traced them in their wanderings to Aird moss, at which place he arrived during the very heat of the engagement. When he approached the desolate and dreary moor, where the combatants were conflicting in deadly strife, he observed a number of persons holding the horses from which the dragoons had dismounted, and guarding their cloaks, which lay in heaps on the edge of the morass. He hastened into the midst of the battle-field, and encountered a gigantic dragoon who was dealing around him many a deadly blow. The fierce dragoon being little accustomed to meet his compeer in single combat, despised his opponent, and, like the proud and vaunting Philistine of Gath, threatened to make his carcass a banquet to the fowls of the air. They fought with equal skill and courage, and for a considerable time it was doubtful who should obtain the victory. At length, however, owing to the unevenness of the ground, the dragoon stumbled, and McMichael embracing the opportunity, pushed him down, and inflicted a mortal wound. The soldier died uttering the most horrid imprecations, and denouncing the unlucky fate that had brought him to his end, by the sword of a detested Covenanter. What a dreadful evil is war! It is one of the most terrible scourges that ever visited this sinful world. In its ravages it has far surpassed famine or pestilence, and has been the means of spreading a wide desolation over the face of the earth, and it has sent millions of souls unprepared into eternity.

No sooner had McMichael performed this part, than he saw that his friends had lost the day, and were fleeing in every direction across the trackless moor. It was now his concern to provide for his own safety; and, having gathered up his armour, he made a speedy retreat from the bloody scene, and returned to his native mountains.

It happened in the course of his wanderings, that on one occasion he paid a visit to his brother Daniel, who informed him of an intended rescue of a number of prisoners who were to be conveyed from Dumfries to Edinburgh to be tried. The projected rescue, it is said, was planned by an individual of the name of Harkness, who had collected several countrymen, who were friendly to the covenanting cause, and willing to risk their lives in the attempt. For this purpose they dug a deep trench on the hills opposite to the path called Enterkin path, along which the dragoons with their prisoners must necessarily proceed, that from this trench, as from a rampart, they might fire suddenly upon the army, and themselves remain in comparative safety. When every thing was prepared,

Harkness who was now impatient for their arrival, set out to reconnoitre, and proceeded onward a few miles in the direction in which he expected them to come; at length he observed the soldiers with the prisoners marching slowly along, and being fully satisfied that they were the party waited for, he retraced his steps with all convenient speed. An individual of the party, however, detected him, and suspecting, from his skulking manner, that he was watching their motions, a detachment was sent in pursuit. He succeeded, however, in making his escape, and left his pursuers entangled in the dangerous intricacies of a deep morass. Having reached the trench in the pass long before the dragoons arrived, he informed his friends of the number of the enemy with whom they expected to cope, and made all suitable preparations for their reception; it was easy to distinguish the prisoners from the soldiers, and, therefore, their aim in firing on them could be taken with perfect precision, and without risk to the former. In a short time the cavalcade was seen winding up the deep and dangerous ravine, dreading no harm, and utterly ununconscious of the fatal ambush that was laid for them. When the party had advanced in a long line exactly opposite the embankment, behind which Harkness and McMichael and their trusty friends had ensconced themselves, the commanding officer was chanting aloud a popular song, which happened to be peculiarly offensive to the Covenanters generally. This circumstance roused the spirit of McMichael, who deemed the song an intolerable insult, and resting his musket on the top of the trench, deliberately pointed a deadly aim at the head of the officer, who tumbled in an instant to the bottom of the ravine. The incident roused the whole party, and made them fully aware of their position. They commenced a vigorous firing, but without effect. No impression was made on the combatants behind the fortification while the soldiers were exposed without a screen to the incessant shots of their opponents. At length, tired out, it would appear, with the unequal contest, the troopers sought safety in flight, and all the prisoners, with one exception, were set at liberty.

The straggling village of Dalry, in Galloway, is situated on the north side of the Ken, on a sunny slope, which terminates in a delightful plain, through which the river pursues its course. It was in this village where the scuffle took place, between the dragoons and some of the peasantry, in the kitchen of the inn, where they accidentally met, and which led to the rising at Pentland, in 1666. In its immediate vicinity is a large moat—the finest, perhaps, in the south of Scotland, used as a meeting place by the ancient Saxons for judicial purposes. Dalry, owing to its situation in a mountainous country, was frequently resorted to by the Covenanters; and formed, like Sanquhar, a kind of central point to the wanderers of the surrounding district. The farm of Stroanpatrick, in the neighbourhood of this village, was, in the times of persecution, tenanted by a person of the name of Roan. This man was professedly a Covenanter, and apparently much attached to the cause. In process of time, however, his fidelity was suspected; and fears were entertained that he was secretly an informer. In reference to this surmise, however, no proof could be distinctly had; but those with whom he was ostensibly connected resolved to investigate the matter, as far as circumstances would permit. Accordingly, McMichael and a few friends were deputed by the societies, or fellowship meetings, as they were called, to converse with Roan on the subject, with power to suspend him as a member of the associations, if the inquiry proved unsatisfactory. These associations, or praying societies, took their rise after the death of Cargill, and were very common during the latter part of the persecuting period. They were of immense advantage in promoting the growth of true religion among the scattered flock of Christ, in the dark and cloudy day of the church's tribulation. They were pools of water in the desert, of which God's heritage often drank and were refreshed. They formed little conventicles without a preacher, in which the word of God was read and commented on by the more aged and experienced members who had the gift of utterance. They were oratories in which prayer, fervent and effectual, was presented to the Father of mercies, for grace to help in time of need, and in which the high praises of God were sung with thankful and adoring hearts. There is no doubt that in these meetings the children of the desert often met with God, and enjoyed a happiness to which their persecutors, who deemed them wretched exiles, were entire strangers. A man's happiness, however, is not to be estimated by external circumstances; for he who outwardly is every thing which one would pronounce blessed, may inwardly be the prey of a misery truly pitiable; while he whose external appearance would indicate much discomfort, may have within him a peace which passeth all understanding. The prayer-meetings which originated among our ancestors, in the times when the preaching of the gospel was rare, have been continued in some of the landward parts till the present day;

and have been upheld by a race of men, who, for intelligence and piety, have but few equals. If prayer-meetings were more common throughout the land, the church of God among us would soon appear to "blossom as the rose;" and a happy change would, ere long, be experienced through the whole Christian community. And it is cheering to witness the impulse that has recently been given to the spirit of social prayer, and to see the goodly number of young praying societies that have lately sprung up among us, both as the means, and as the fruits of a religious revival.

The deputation, then, from the societies, met with Roan, and strictly interrogated him respecting the rumour of his defection, and traitorous correspondence with the enemy. Roan affirmed that the report was false, and that he was as true to the good cause as ever. He admitted that soldiers had frequently come to his house inquiring after Covenanters; but that no information whatever had at any time been imparted by him. His averments were not fully credited, for there appeared something confused and hesitating about his manner. McMichael stated that, as they were by no means satisfied with his attempted exculpation, they were resolved to exercise the authority conferred on them by the associations, of interdicting his attendance on their meetings, until he had clearly purged himself of the accusation of being a spy and an informer; and that, in the mean time, he must deliver up his arms. The place where this interview was held was at some distance from Stroanpatrick, at which place Roan said his arms were deposited; and to this place he requested them to proceed, that there they might receive them from his own hand. It had been observed by one of the party, that, during the unsatisfactory examination of their suspected associate, their leader's eye was beginning to kindle; and, fearing lest some untoward incident might befal, he stole to the door where their fire-arms were leaning against the wall, and extracted the shot from McMichael's musket. The party then set out for Stroanpatrick. The road to this place passed through a broad meadow, through the midst of which flowed a small stream. As they were proceeding along the meadow, and near the banks of the streamlet, Roan, watching his opportunity, darted from his companions, and sprang over the brook, with evident intention of deserting the party. Suspicion was roused, and it appeared plain to every one that their associate was a traitor. McMichael fired, but without effect. The alarmed fugitive fled with winged speed, and McMichael, with his sword drawn, pursued; and, when he found that he was not gaining ground in the pursuit, he flung after him, with all his might, the glittering blade, which smote him with such force that it inflicted a mortal wound, and he bled to death on the spot. Thus ended the mission on which McMichael and his fellows were sent: it terminated disastrously for the poor man to whom suspicion attached, and not very creditably to those who were commissioned to remonstrate with him on the alleged dishonesty of his conduct. The deed, on the part of McMichael, was rash and unwarranted, and deserved the severest reprehension: it is revolting to a serious mind, and a deed, on account of which its perpetrator would no doubt feel some compunctious visitings. It is probable, however, that McMichael did not intend to kill the man, but only to disable, and to prevent him from doing the mischief which in all likelihood he intended. This supposition receives countenance from the fact, that James McMichael aimed his blow at the lower part of his body, where he actually struck the blow which unintentionally, we hope issued in his death.

Peter Pierson, the Curate of Carsfairn, was, like many of his brethren, an object of special dislike to the neighbourhood in which he resided. He entered fully into the spirit of the party with which he was connected, and was unwearied in his search after nonconformists in his parish, and punctual in communicating information respecting them. He cherished, as might be expected, a cordial dislike to the Covenanters; and was constantly taking account of those of his parishioners who refused to attend his church. His interference in this way became at length absolutely intolerable, and the people were determined to submit no longer. Accordingly a party, of which McMichael formed one, proceeded to the manse, with a view to remonstrate with the Curate; and, if possible, to bring him to a better understanding. They had drawn up a paper, to the requisitions contained in which they desired of him an express and unequivocal agreement. They informed him that the chief thing that they wanted of him was, that he should allow them to live without molestation in reference to religious matters; and that, if this proposition was agreed to, they would give him no more trouble. When the purport of this interview was made known he became greatly enraged, and would listen to nothing they had to say. On the arrival of the party at the manse, it was agreed that a few of their number should station themselves at the door to keep watch, while the rest entered the house. When the men entered the

Curate's apartment, and made known their errand he barred the door, and presented a loaded pistol to shoot the intruders on the spot. The men without, hearing the uproar, and the cries of their friends for assistance, demanded an instant admit tance. On entering the room, McMichael, seeing the perilous circumstances of his companions, and the danger in which he himself was now placed, in the hastiness of his spirit fired, and the Curate fell dead on the floor. His associates, when they first perceived his intention, commanded him to desist; but he heeded them not. This deed, which McMichael with a reckless hand perpetrated, was highly disapproved of by the Covenanters in the south-west of Scotland. It was not their wish to shed blood, but rather, by all honest means, to prevent its effusion; and the societies having taken the matter into consideration, resolved on the expulsion of McMichael from their associations, because the killing of the Curate was, in their estimation, an action which could not be justified. It does not appear, however, that McMichael had any intention of injuring the incumbent, further than what might befal in mere self-defence. His own life, and the life of his companions, was threatened by a vengeful and turbulent man, whose constant work was, by all means, to harass and persecute the people of God, who were willing to live peaceably, and to do injury to no man. That such a man was, on the present occasion, about to shoot some of the party, there can be no doubt; and it was not to be expected that a man of McMichael's temper would calmly wait the catastrophe. That McMichael committed a grievous error cannot be questioned, especially when we consider that the number present in the chamber was sufficient to disarm the Curate, without offering violence to his person. The unhappy man, however, lost his life, and lost it as the agent of a very sinful faction, and was therefore the less prepared for entering eternity. Incidents of this kind, instead of alleviating, aggravated the sufferings of the Covenanters; and the guilt of what was done privately, and by a few on their own responsibility, was charged on the whole body, and afforded their adversaries a pretext for rendering the persecution still more general and severe. The societies, by their expulsion of McMichael, showed that they were not connected with this deed, and that it was a step which they repudiated. Whether they saw reason afterwards to admit him, tradition does not say; but their sentiments, expressed in this way, were calculated to produce a salutary impression on the mind of one whose impetuosity of temper carried him occasionally far beyond the bounds of propriety.*

Those who are of an irritable disposition have much need to exercise watchfulness, lest Satan take occasion of their infirmity to hurry them into acts of sin which may grieve the Holy Spirit, dishonour their Christian profession, and wring their own hearts with regret till their dying day. Believers should reflect that there is no feature of the Christian character so amiable, and so much in keeping with the gospel temper, as a meek and quiet spirit. "Learn of me, for I am meek and lowly in heart, and ye shall find rest unto your souls." Peace cannot dwell in a heart that is constantly fretted with angry passions, and in which the least provo-

*[The conduct of McMichael in this and a former instance, deserves a much more severe reprobation than the author seems disposed to give it. *Editor of the Presbyterian Board.*]

cation excites wrathful emotions. Anger, frequently indulged, becomes at length a disease of the mind, which nothing but the all-powerful grace of God can cure. Few persons seem to be more unfit for that heaven where all is love, and peace, and serenity, than those who indulge a turbulent and irascible temper. "But the fruit of the Spirit is love, joy, peace, *long-suffering*, *gentleness*, goodness, *meekness*." There is, however, no evil habit, nor passion, which may not be subdued, and which will not be subdued, if by faith we take hold of the strength of Him who is able to crush all our spiritual enemies under our feet. It is a noble display of the real efficacy of Divine grace when it is seen mollifying and sweetening the temper that was formerly rough and indomitable, and changing the wolf into the lamb. Not to speak of the greater mischiefs which the proud and overbearing tempers of men have produced in society at large, let us look to the heart-burnings and the discomfort among neighbours, and in families, of which peevishness and irritability, not religiously counteracted are the cause. A fretful disposition, like a canker, corrodes the heart, and leaves it solitary and wretched. "He that hath no rule over his own spirit is like a city that is broken down and without walls."

After the death of Pierson the curate, McMichael, though in the mean time expelled by the societies, still adhered with unflinching constancy to the cause of civil and religious freedom. He was now under the necessity of using greater caution in his movements, and of retiring more frequently to the desolate parts of the country. His enemies now considered him as a person of some consequence, and were therefore determined to apprehend him. Claverhouse, with his troopers, had entered the district where he was suspected to be lurking, and was using every means to get him and his associates into his power. At this time McMichael and several of his companions were concealed among the hills, near the Water of Dee; and Claverhouse, having received information of the circumstance, surprised them in their hiding place at a moment when they dreaded no harm. The sudden onslaught threw the party at first into confusion, and two of their number fled unnoticed into a shepherd's hut; but the others, finding no way of escape, were obliged to stand on the defensive. The skirmish was severe; both parties were brave, and fought with courage. Claverhouse advanced on McMichael, sword in hand, in the full confidence of gaining an easy conquest. That haughty soldier feared no danger, and seldom met with his equal on the battle-field. In the person of McMichael, however, he found a warrior who, in point of martial dexterity and true heroism, was not inferior to himself; and long and stiffly was the combat maintained, till Claverhouse, dreading the consequences, called out lustily for assistance. "You dare not," cried McMichael, "abide the issue of a single combat; and had your helmet been like mine, a soft bonnet, your carcass had ere this found its bed on the heath!" The dispute, however, was soon terminated, for a powerful dragoon approaching cautiously, came behind McMichael, and with one stroke of his ponderous blade clave his head in two. Thus fell a leal-hearted patriot, whose prowess the most illustrious cavalier of his time feared to withstand, and whose conduct, where it is culpable, is more to be attributed to the times than to the man. It is easy for us, in the full enjoyment of that civil liberty which the struggles of these very men have bequeathed to us, to speculate on their conduct, and to praise or to blame, where, in the plenitude of our superior wisdom and prudence, we may find convenient; but had we now the same work to perform, and the same afflictions to endure, it is questionable if in any respect we would act a better part, or even our part half so well. McMichael was both a Christian and a patriot; and while tradition has preserved more of his patriotism than his Christianity—which can easily be accounted for, owing to the part which he was called to act—this does not prove any decided inferiority to the worthies of that trying time, nor any remarkable deficiency in what constitutes "the highest style of man." Of the few that were with McMichael, two were killed, and one severely wounded. When the dragoons were going to despatch the wounded man, Claverhouse requested them to stay till he made some inquiries respecting the death of the Curate. The dying man replied, that the divulging of that circumstance could now do no harm, as the man who had done that deed—pointing to the body of McMichael—was beyond the reach of his enemies. On this the soldiers thrust their swords through the dead body, and then suspended it ignominiously on a tree. Not long after, a number of the country people who respected the memory of McMichael came, like the men of Jabesh-Gilead, who stole the dishonoured body of Saul from the wall of Bethshan, and buried the remains of their friend, who had asserted their liberties at the cost of his own life, in a place which is said not now to be known.

The killing of James McMichael and his companions by Claverhouse on the Water of Dee, is similar to the account given by Wodrow of the slaughter of one James McMichan and his companions by Claverhouse, in the same place; and the statement of the circumstances seems to be nearly the same. The confusion, perhaps, has arisen from the similarity of the names; for McMichael and McMichan sound very much alike. The death of McMichan, however, was in 1684, and the killing of the Curate of Carsfairn was in 1685, and it is probable that McMichael was killed in the same year. Besides Daniel, who was shot at Dalveen, James McMichael seems to have had another brother of the name of Gilbert, who appears to have been a man of uncommon piety and Christian attainment. He died on his bed full of spiritual consolation and heavenly hope; and though he attained not to the honour of martyrdom, yet his name is enrolled among the witnessing remnant whom Christ will honour as those who, for his sake, loved not their lives unto the death.

CHAPTER V.

Peden—Castle Gilmour—Auchentagart—Elliock—Glen quhary Cleuch.

In a former chapter it was remarked that Mr. Peden had, according to tradition, in the forest of Glendyne near Sanquhar, a retreat to which he sometimes resorted in his wanderings, and in the neighbourhood of which he was favoured with a special interposition of Providence, in his being screened from the view of his persecutors by means of a dense mist which descended from the hills, and covered him, and the few that were with him, when they were fleeing for their lives. This occurrence is related by old Patrick Walker in the following words: "After this, in Auchengrouch muirs in Nithsdale, Captain John Mathison and others being with him, they were alarmed with a report that the enemy were coming fast upon him, so they designed to put him in some hole, and cover him with heather. But he not being able to run hard by reason of age, he desired them to forbear a little until he prayed, when he said, "Lord, we are ever needing at thy hand, and if we had not thy command to call upon thee in the day of our trouble, and thy promise of answering us in the day of our distress, we wot not what would become of us; if thou hast any more work for us in thy world, allow us the lap of thy cloak this day again; and if this be the day of our going off the stage, let us walk honestly off, and comfortably thorow, and our souls will sing forth thy praises to eternity for what thou hast done to us, and for us." When ended he ran alone a little, and came quickly back, saying, "Lads, the bitterest of this blast is over; we will be no more troubled with them this day." Foot and horse came the length of Andrew Clark's, in Auchengrouch, where they were covered with a dark mist. When they saw it they roared like fleshly devils, as they were crying out, "There 's the confounded mist again! we cannot get these execrable whigs pursued for it." I had these accounts from the said Captain John Mathison." Such is the statement of the incident given by Walker; the local tradition, however, is much more circumstantial.

Castle Gilmour, as its name imports, was an old baronial residence in the moors, about three miles to the east of Sanquhar, and is now a modern farm-house. The locality must in ancient times have been very dreary and desolate, for even yet its general aspect is any thing but interesting. The mountains, however, by which it is encompassed on the east and on the north, are of a very different description. Few scenes, on a narrow scale, present a more agreeable spectacle than that which meets the view from the northern limits of Sanquhar town common, between the parallel streams of Menock and the Crawick. The uncultivated moorlands are flanked by hills whose summits rise like lofty colonnades to the clouds, and remind one of the sublime Scripture expression, "the pillars of heaven." The beautiful Knockenhair, in the western corner of the circular range, clad in velvet green, and topped with its ancient warder cairn, stands a stately cone detached from the neighbouring mountains, and, presenting itself in advance, invites the first glance of the spectator's eye. In the eastern corner stands the gray-clothed height of Auchengrouch, the frequent sanctuary of the worthy Peden, and to which the memory of that venerable saint has imparted a hallowed interest. The traveller in the bleak dale land which stretches from the base of these mountains to the south, often meets with the plover and the peeweep, which in their aerial gyrations, dive downwards, and flap with their broad wings his head and shoulders, as a chastisement for intruding on their solitary retreats. In this way, it is said, they were occasionally unconscious informers to the enemy of the wanderers who, in the open field, had concealed themselves in the heart of the bracken bush, or among the green coverts of the matted grass. In the stillness of a sweet summer evening, when, in meditative mood, one surveys the entire scene, and gathers in all its associations, there is felt a kind of enchantment, which one is unwilling to dissipate. We think on the incidents of former times; we reflect on the wanderings and the prayers of our suffering forefathers, who made the solitudes their home, and who, when furthest from men, were nearest God. We think on the times of a still more remote ancestry, and picture the ancient Celtic people who claimed these mountains and wilds as their own, and who traversed these territories as free and as light as the fitful breeze that streams along the heath; and we ruminate on times that are yet to come, when righteous generations shall arise, for whose sake God will remove the curse from the barren wilderness; and when, under the culture of their skilful hands, that same desert, over which the eye roams, will "rejoice and blossom as the rose." An age of millennial blessedness shall arrive, in which changes and improvements shall take place, of which we have little anticipation. But we who live shall have passed away with the former generations that are already in the dust, and our eyes shall not behold among the living the goodness which God has provided for those who shall come after, and whom he will render more worthy of its enjoyments than we are. If, however, our hope be in heaven, and if, after death our souls have their dwelling there, we shall enjoy a better millennium, and a higher blessedness, than they of earth can boast of. Only be it our care to secure, by faith in the Redeemer, an entrance into that rest which remaineth for the people of God, and then we shall have occasion to sing, "O how great is thy goodness which thou hast laid up for them that fear thee, which thou hast wrought for them that trust in thee before the sons of men '"

It was in the farm-house of Castle Gilmour, in the immediate vicinity of Auchengrouch, where Mr. Peden and a few friends had taken refuge. In their wandering in the moors they were overcome with fatigue and hunger; and to this friendly house they came seeking rest and refreshment. Andrew Clark in Auchengrouch was a good man, a zealous Covenanter; and one who readily afforded shelter to the outcasts; and it seems that his neighbour in Castle Gilmour was no less attached to the good cause, and no less hospitable to those who were suffering for Christ's sake. On the farm of Castle Gilmour, the dwelling-house and offices were so constructed as to form an exact square, with openings at the corners, through which one individual or two could pass at a time. Mr. Peden and his friends were partaking of a repast after their long fasting; and, dreading no harm, were discoursing freely on the subjects that were most interesting to them, when, to their surprise, and without the least warning, a company of dragoons rode into the enclosure before the dwelling-house, and drew up at the door. The party within, seeing no way of escape except in the very face of the enemy, made a simultaneous rush to the door, and waving with their bonnets, ran here and there among the horses before the riders got time to dismount, and escaped every one of them through the narrow passages at the angles of the square. The troopers were confounded at an occurrence so un expected; for they, thinking that their prey was sure, were very much at their ease, and were making no great haste to enter the house. The dragoons, when they understood the true position of matters, and having learned that the persons whc had just now issued with so much impetuosity and disorder from the dwelling-house, were the very individuals of whom they were in quest, wheeled round, and departing by the way they entered, pursued with all speed. Meanwhile the fugitives had reached Auchengrouch burn, and arrived at the other side in safety. This was a great point gained; for the place at which they passed the stream was so precipitous, that the horsemen could not follow them. By the time, then, that they emerged on the opposite bank, the troopers, in full chase, were close to the brook ; but their progress was instantly arrested by the descent, down which the horses could not march. The shots which they fired across the little ravine took no effect; and the covenanting friends pursued their way along the heath, to where Providence might be pleased to guide them. The soldiers, however, were not to be baffled by the obstacles which now crossed their path ; and turning in another direction, cleared the bent with all the speed its rugged surface would permit, and were fast gaining ground. The fleeing party now perceived that there was little likelihood of escape. Mr. Peden, whose refuge in the midst of his distresses was prayer, and who used to remark that "it was only praying people that would get through the storm," requested the company to halt a little till he prayed, which he did in the words recorded by Walker, and then he added, "Lads, the bitterest of this blast is over, we will be no more troubled with them this day." The occasion of their rescue was the mist which descended from the hills, and screened them from the view of their pursuers.

Some may be inclined to suppose that this incident is put forth as something miraculous, and to say that the admission of a miracle vitiates the entire statement. There is, however, no occasion whatever to suppose a miracle in this, more than in other providential interferences in answer to prayer. Are we to say, that the Divine Being cannot in any case answer our prayers, in reference to external deliverances, without a miracle? The settling of the mist on the tops of these mountains, is a very common occurrence, and could not He who "maketh the clouds his chariot, and who walketh upon the wings of the wind," in answer to the prayer of his servant, in the day of his distress, send a stream of air from the mountain side, and spread the misty covering over his people who trusted in him, without the introduction of a miracle? Some again may be inclined to consider the thing as a mere coincidence; but the question is, who appointed the coincidence, or was it merely fortuitous, a thing of chance? and had the great Disposer of events no hand in it? No person will admit this who believes the Scripture-doctrine of a providence, of a particular providence exercised over all creatures and all events. "Are not two sparrows sold for a farthing, and one of them shall not fall on the ground without your Father; but the very hairs of your head are all numbered." Nor will they who believe in the efficacy of prayer be disposed to deny that the incident was really in answer to prayer: "Call upon me in the day of trouble; I will deliver thee, and thou shalt glorify me." An infidel will no doubt laugh at this, but a serious Christian will rejoice in the fact that the Lord hears prayer, and that he is prompt to answer it. Prayer is a means of attaining an end, and if the end has a place in the Divine appointment, so has the means, and the former is not to be obtained without the latter. The people of God believe the Bible doctrine respecting prayer, both as a duty to be performed, and as an instrument of obtaining blessings: "Ask, and ye shall receive." How much do they lose who restrain prayer before God; and what a difference in point of success in prayer is there between the man who prays with a weak and faltering confidence, and the man who prays in strong faith! The one receives blessings, copious as the showers which descend from the teeming firmament, when the windows of heaven are opened; and what the other receives is only like the scanty rain dripping reluctantly from the skirts of a transient cloud. We are bound to believe, that when we ask blessings from God in the name of Christ, we shall receive them: "For this is the confidence that we have in him, that if we ask any thing according to his will, he heareth us;" and "he that cometh unto God, must believe that he is, and that he is the rewarder of them that diligently seek him." Here then, the secret of success in prayer, is the *confidence* that our prayers shall be heard for Christ's sake; for he that prays and believes, is answered, while he that prays and believes not, is not answered.

The farm-house of Auchentagart, which is in the vicinity of Castle Gilmour, was also, in the days of persecution, a place of refuge to the wanderers. The name of the place is Celtic, and signifies "the field of the priest." From this it would appear that the ancient Celtic people had somewhere in this locality a church, to which the lands of Auchentagart were attached—a proof that the gospel in remote times was introduced into the neighbourhood, and that God was here worshipped by the people of a forgotten age, in a house of which there is not the least trace nor tradition. It is pleasant to think that the ancient inhabitants of this country, long prior to the times of Romish superstition, enjoyed a pure dispensation of divine grace, and were in these times brought to the knowledge of the truth.

It happened one day that a few of the covenanting friends entered the house of Auchentagart, where they were cordially welcomed by its master, for the sake of Him in whose cause they were suffering hardship. As there were more households than one in this moorland part, who kindly entertained the houseless wanderers, the dragoons must therefore have been more frequently seen traversing the waste, and strolling from one hiding-place to another, for the purpose of seizing, in cave or shiel, any who might perchance be concealed in these retreats. In their ramblings from place to place, they were, on the very day on which the friends had taken refuge in Auchentagart, observed coming across the moor, straight to the house. It was obvious that a visit was intended; and that the soldiers, if meeting with no adventure in the way of their profession, would in all likelihood demand entertainment, both for themselves and their horses, and probably spend the greater part of the day on the premises. On the first appearance of the party, information was hastily communicated to the few refugees, who were receiving refreshment within. They instantly left the house, and fled in the direction of the wood of Glendyne. Their flight, however, was observed by the troopers, who immediately commenced a pursuit, but were not able to overtake them. It would appear, that the dragoons had, in sallying out on this occasion, a double object in view; they were prepared for sport as well as for persecution, for hunting the timid hare as well as for pursuing men, and were accompanied with a pack of powerful and cruel dogs. These dogs they sent in chase of the fleeing Covenanters, and they tracked their path with fleetness and voracity to the mouth of the woody glen, into which the fugitives plunged and concealed themselves, before their canine pursuers could overtake them. In this retreat they were safe, and were left without interruption, to render a grateful acknowledgment to Him who had once more shielded them in the time of danger. The tradition that some of these dogs were bloodhounds, and that their progress was arrested by the circumstance of one of the party having drawn blood from his hand with a view to weaken the scent, is not tenable, for reasons that could be easily assigned. One is ready to blush for human nature, when one class of men are seen employing in this way animals to pursue another, as if they were beasts of prey, fit only to be torn in pieces by the fangs of the huntsman's dog. To such degradation, however, and even to worse, have the people of God been subjected in the treatment which they have received from their enemies. They have been regarded as 'the filth of the world, and as the offscouring of all things;' but while they were thus disesteemed by men, they were honoured of God, and they deemed themselves happy in being counted worthy to be reproached and maltreated for his name.

The beautiful lands of Elliock lie opposite to Castle Gilmour, and about two miles to the south of Sanquhar. Elliock House is couched in the midst of a pleasant wood. It is an edifice, part of which boasts a considerable antiquity, being preserved as the birth-place of the Admirable Crichton, notwithstanding the claims which another place has laid to this distinguished honour, as seven cities contended for the birth of Homer. In former times it was the property of the Earl of Carnwath, who in the days of our persecuted ancestors sided with their oppressors. Elliock house was therefore a station for the dragoons, who accompanied the Earl in his movements through the country for the purpose of subduing a rebellious peasantry. It was not, however, the only station in this vicinity; for both the town of Sanquhar, and its neighbouring castle, must have been the receptacles of a soldiery who were employed to murder their countrymen for the offence of yielding an honest obedience to the Divine law in preference to the iniquitous impositions of men. The garrison at Elliock, then, were ready at a moment's warning to scour the Highlands that lay to the south, and that stretched along the desert moorlands that reached the Scar; and as there was a constant intercourse between the higher parts of Galloway and the upper ward of Lanarkshire by way of Sanquhar, the services of the soldiers would be in perpetual demand. On the north, Elliock commanded a view of all that was in motion along the line of the Nith, and on the green heights that overlook the highway, so that, in this direction, nothing could escape the vigilance of the warders who might be set to give due notice of what was passing. It was observed in a former paper, that a number of those who were friendly to the Covenanters connected themselves with the royal forces for the express purpose of defeating the plans of the enemy, and of giving warning to the persecuted when danger was near; and the following anecdote of one of the dragoons at Elliock House is illustrative of the fact. One evening the commander gave orders to the troopers to hold themselves in readiness for a raid on the morrow, without specifying the particular quarter to which he intended to proceed. Every man was instantly on the alert, and saw that his ammunition, and his musket, and his sword, and his charger, were all in readiness for the intended sally in the morning. On the grounds of Elliock, on the border of the heath, lived a venerable matron, a mother in Israel, whose name tradition has not preserved, the door of whose house was always open to the helpless wanderer. This woman had often entertained and sheltered those who, for their Maker's sake, had suffered the loss of all things. At the peril of her life, and of all she held dear in this world, she ventured to perform what she reckoned a duty to the followers of Christ in the day of their calamity; and she was blessed in her deed—for Providence shielded her from harm, and even prevented suspicion from lighting upon her as one who dared to harbour, or in any way to assist those who were so obnoxious to the ruling powers. This appears the more remarkable, considering her abode was so near the head-quarters of the troopers, who, in their idle hours, must have been constantly strolling about the neighbourhood, and prying with an impertinent curiosity into every corner, and every house, and that with the full license, in many cases, to act as they pleased. There was one of the soldiers, however, who was acquainted with her house, and who had some knowledge of the kind of persons who often gathered around its hearth. This man, after the orders were issued by his officers, stole unperceived, under the cloud of night, to the cottage on the moor. "Mistress," said he, "I am come to warn you, we are to be *out* to-morrow, and we may perhaps pass your way; if you have any friends about you at present, I give you the watchword that they may provide for their safety, and take care of yourself. Good night." Whether there were any under hiding at this time in her house is not said; but the knowledge that, when practicable, she would receive information of approaching danger, must have kept her mind at ease, and rendered her abode a retreat of comparative security; and the soldier, whether he acted from a mere impulse of humanity, or from real principle, must have had a peculiar satisfaction, in knowing that he had been the instrument of shielding from danger a company of worthy men, who had by no means merited the severe treatment to which they were subjected. It is impossible to say of how much use a man or two of this description, in a troop of dragoons, must have been to the cause of the suffering party; and it is not easy to calculate the amount of mischief which, in the localities where they were stationed, they must have occasionally prevented. One friend in the enemy's camp is sometimes worth a thousand men in the field.

There lived on the same lands of Elliock, at this period, a pious man of the name of Baird, who in the heat of the persecution, fled from his residence in Glenmuir water, in Kyle. He was a man of great worth, and was much befriended by the persons who were favourable to the cause of the persecuted. He died in this place, and was interred in the ancient burying-ground of Kirkbride. His son married a daughter of Adam Clark, nephew of Andrew Clark of Auchengrouch, mentioned by Patrick Walker. This Andrew Clark, who was a noted Covenanter, had no fewer than nine sons, all of whom firmly embraced their father's principles. An anecdote is told of this Adam Clark, who lived at Glenim, a retired spot among the hills, a short distance to the east of the delightful valley of Menok. A party of dragoons was sent one day to Glenim for the purpose of apprehending Robert; he happened to meet them at the door of his house, and, having accosted them in a rude, and, as they thought, a profane manner, they concluded that he was not the kind of person that he was represented to be, else he would not have employed language which did not seem to befit the mouth of a Covenanter; and, without more ado, they left the place. His friends, it is said, were much displeased with his conduct on this occasion; but he justified himself on the ground that his words had saved both himself and them. What the exact words were, is not distinctly known: but is is probable, though they savoured somewhat of the loose style of the dragoons, that there was in reality little profanity in them. It is related of a worthy minister, in those times of ecclesiastical oppression, who was sought for in the house of a friend, that he escaped by vociferating in the ears of the uproarious soldiery, "I dare say the *devil* is in these people!" This exclamat.on was deemed profane, and the enemies who came in search of him allowed him to pass through the midst of them unharmed. What this good man said was true; but because he used the devil's name, in whose service they were engaged, in what they thought an unguarded and irreverent manner, they deemed him no better than themselves, and hence they did not suspect him to be the person whom they wanted. It is a species of the grossest profanity, and even blasphemy, to place, as some ignorantly do, the devil's name on a level with the Divine name; and to suppose it to be as great an evil to use the one in conversation as the other. This is truly rendering a homage to Satan in which he must rejoice. The devil is but a creature, and his name may be used as that of any other creature; but not so "this glorious and fearful name, *The Lord thy God.*" We must not swear by the name of any creature, for that is expressly forbidden in the Scriptures; but to hold the name of Satan as sacred as the name of God is certainly a fearful impiety.

The parish of Kirkconnel, which is contiguous to Sanquhar on the west, was, in the time of the persecution, frequently subjected, as Wodrow shows, to the ravages of an unprincipled soldiery. Claverhouse, in his raids, sometimes scoured both sides of the river, and carried off numbers both of men and women. It appears that Glenquhary cleuch in this parish, above Kirkland, and a little to the west of the beautiful valley of Glen Aylmer, was an occasional haunt of the Covenanters. Glenquhary heights command on the south an extensive view of the delightful vale of the Nith; and, on the north, they overlook one of the most perfect solitudes in nature, and a solitude of vast extent, reaching forward to Glenmuir water, whose valley has been rendered interesting by the classic strains of the "Cameronian's Dream:"*

"In Glenmuir's wild solitudes lengthened and deep
Were the whistling of plovers and bleating of sheep."

The author of this exquisite poem lived, when a boy, in the midst of this sequestered glen, at a place called Dalblair, where his fine poetic genius was stimulated and nurtured by the mingled scenes of soft beauty and wild grandeur with which he was surrounded. Glenmuir-shaw, near the head of this valley is a pleasant spot; and must, in former times, have been a place of some consequence, as the ruins of its ancient baronial castle still indicate. Some lordly chieftain of the Saxon line seems to have selected it as the locality in which he chose to live in a state of rude splendour; and which must have been witnessed by the lonely sentinels that still guard the spot—the stately trees, whose dotard boughs and scaly rind bespeak the age of several centuries. He who sighs after a sweet meditative seclusion, will find that seclusion at Glenmuir-shaw.

Glenquhary cleuch is a retired and deep recess among the mountains, and a locality extremely favourable to those who were under hiding, on account of the facilities it afforded of escape to the hills, and to the dreary desert that lay beyond. On one occasion a company of Covenanters had taken refuge in this romantic cleft, and which, by them, was converted into a temple as well as an asylum. It appears that certain suspicions of their being convened in this retreat were entertained by the enemy, who one evening held a consultation, and came to the determination to institute, on the morrow, a strict search, beginning at Glenquhary cleuch, and proceeding along the line of mountains to the point of Corsancone, and thence passing to the south side of the river, to steal along the valley of the Afton in the direction of Carsfairn; and in this way to apprehend as many as they could find.

One of the dragoons, when he understood the work in which he, in common with his fellows, was to be employed in the morning, felt some compunctious visitings, which ultimately threw him into great mental distress. He arose in the dead of night, and having determined to abandon his wicked occupation, he proceeded straight to the cleuch in search of the refugees. He informed them of their impending danger, and revealed to them the state of his mind, and the resolution to which he had come. He was cordially received by the party, who agreed instantly to set out, and give warning to their brethren in all their hiding-places, along the tract in which the dragoons intended to march on the following day. It was in this way that Providence shielded from harm many a helpless and unsuspecting household, who probably, at this very time, had been led to repose a more than ordinary confidence in God's protecting care: and who, in answer to their prayers, were made to witness a more than common interposition in their favour. The deliverance came from the enemy's own camp; and one of themselves, whose heart God had touched, was made the instrument of defeating their own purposes. It is to be hoped that the poor soldier, who had begun to see the evil of his conduct, was led, by the instructions and the prayers of his new associates, to the knowledge of the truth. He was the means of saving their lives: and they, perhaps, were the means of saving his soul. The disappointment of the dragoons when next day they rode their round, without, in any instance, gaining their object, must have been great; and their surprise at the desertion of their comrade must have been equally great. The little company who, in the dark night, had taken shelter in the cleuch, did not think it enough to provide for their own safety by timely evacuating their hiding-place, they were equally concerned for the safety of their brethren, who lay in the line of the projected route; and they considered no toil too much to rescue them from the common danger.

CHAPTER VI.

William Swan—Scene in the Barn—Cave at the Crags—Conventicle at Wardlaw—Search for Arms—Incident.

THE house of Braehead in Dalswinton is situated on a rising ground, commanding an extensive pros pect of the country around, and especially of the vale beneath. This place, in the time of the persecution, was tenanted by a worthy person of the name of Swan. William Swan was a person devoted to the covenanting cause, and no less devoted to the cause of godliness. No heart beat with a kindlier feeling to those who were suffering for righteousness sake, than did the heart of this honest man; and no door was opened with a more cordial welcome than his to admit the homeless wanderer. His mind was no less active than his heart was generous; active in devising expedients for the purpose of concealing, without the risk of discovery, those who fled to his friendly mansion for refuge. In his barn he formed a hiding-place for the reception of those who, knowing his readiness to assist the oppressed, flocked to him in considerable numbers. This hiding-place was an open space which was left between the wall and the corn-sheaves or the hay, which was built up from the floor to the roof, with a small entrance at one corner, which was closed so accurately as not to be perceptible. The vacancy behind was so large as to admit a goodly number of persons together; and it is said that he sometimes had no fewer than a score of individuals in this receptacle at once, who under his guardian care, felt themselves as secure as in a castle. These persons he fed at his own expense, as the good Obadiah did the prophets of the Lord in a cave; and William Swan rejoiced in the exercise of an ample hospitality toward those who were subject to hunger and destitution for Christ's sake. And doubtless he experienced the truth of our Lord's saying—"It is more blessed to give than to receive." They who give for the truth's sake give unto the Lord, and he will repay; and he often repays in *kind:* "The liberal soul shall be made fat; and he that watereth shall be watered also himself. This little chamber in the barn was converted into a church, where these devout worshippers of God often refreshed themselves in the performance of religious exercises; and lest, on these occasions, they should be surprised by their enemies when the loud voice of their united praises might perchance escape beyond the walls of their narrow cell, giving intimation to those who were without, of what was going on within, he made use of a particular sign by which he cautiously communicated warning when danger was near. In his immediate neighbourhood there lived a dangerous man of the name of Cowan. This man was by trade a turner and an infamous informer, who received the payment of a pound for every individual he betrayed to the government. It was the interest of William Swan, for his own sake, and for the sake of those whom he occasionally concealed in his house, to use every means to lull the suspicions of this person, and to gain, as far as possible, his good will by the liberal bestowment of valuable presents. In this way a kindly feeling was, to a certain degree, wrought in the breast of Cowan, who, in order to show his respect for Swan, presented him with a little table made of oak, and finished according to the best style of his trade, and which is to this day preserved as an heirloom by the descendants of William Swan. Thus, "when a man's ways please the Lord, he maketh even his enemies to be at peace with him." Cowan had it in his power to do much mischief; but Providence, by the means specified, was pleased to restrain that power, and the bone that was thrown to the dog prevented his barking.

But William Swan, with all his caution, could not prevent an occasional visit of the enemy. He was suspected of harbouring the intercommuned, as they were called, and one day a party of dragoons were sent to search the premises. Their approach was first noticed by his wife, who, in great consternation, communicated the circumstance to her husband, who had at this time about twenty of the sufferers concealed behind the *mow*, for whose safety he was much concerned. His fertile mind, however, instantly suggested an expedient which, in the result, proved successful in accomplishing their deliverance. He had at this time a great quantity of wool piled up in the end of the barn, opposite the place where the friends were concealed behind the hay. He took his wife into the barn, and explained to her in the hearing of the company, who were in the hiding-place, the manner in which, in the present emergency, he intended to act. It was his design, he said, to be apparently engaged in severe altercation with her when the soldiers arrived, respecting part of the wool which he was to suppose had been abstracted from the heap, and, under that pretence, to lock the door in the face of the dragoons to prevent the intrusion of thieves. The plan having been agreed to, they waited with no little anxiety the arrival of the horsemen, who were just at hand. As they turned into the space before the door the loud voice of William Swan was heard rising in angry tones above the clattering of the horses' feet on the pavement, as they rushed forward to the scene of strife within the barn. "I will not permit you, my wife though you be," vociferated Swan, "I will not allow you, nor any one else, to set a foot on the floor of this barn so long as my wool lies here. Take that," rolling a fleece in his arms and throwing it at her, "take that, and make what use of it you please, and be gone." He then drove his wife from the place as if she had been a thief, and stepping out after her, closed the door with violence and locked it, and then, with apparent rage, and firm determination, exclaimed, "Let me see the person who will dare to enter this barn without my permission." If the soldiers were astonished, we may conclude they were equally amused, for a scene of this kind could not fail to afford men in their situation much merriment. The scheme, however, was successful, and the dragoons, without making any investigation whatever, marched off under the impression that the information respecting Swan was false. With regard to the propriety of his procedure in this case, that is another matter; the plan, perhaps, was neither the most judicious nor the most praiseworthy. It was, however, a difficult matter for a man in his situation to know how to act, and he adopted what on the spur of the moment appeared to him to be the most eligible method.

Near the water of Ae, between the parishes of Kirkmahoe and Tinwald, is a place called the Crags, in which there was a cave which, like many other places of a similar description in the wilder parts of the country, was resorted to by those who sought concealment from their enemies. This place was well known to William Swan, who did not fail to minister to the wants of those who had taken refuge in its cold and cheerless recesses. The hospitality of this excellent man was not confined simply to those who sought an asylum in his own house; it extended to all within his reach, whether they were hidden in the moss, or in the wood, or in the cave. There is a largeness of heart, and an expansive generosity of soul, which characterize some good men, assimilating them more than others to the image of Him who is goodness itself. We respect a just man, and we esteem a righteous man, but we *love* a good man: his affectionate sympathy, and the assiduity of his kindness, bind our hearts to him with the tie of a particular attachment, and we contemplate his character with a sweet complacency. One day after dinner, and thanks returned to Him who fills all his creatures with plenteousness, William Swan was reposing in his arm-chair, and musing with a grateful heart on the benignity of that Providence that had 'prepared a table before him in the presence of his enemies;' he remembered his brethren in affliction, the sufferers who were in concealment in the cave at the Crags, and he felt as if the bountiful meal which he had now received would do him little good unless they too were made sharers of the same provision. "My dear family," said he, "we have participated amply of our heavenly Father's bounty, and we are strengthened and refreshed; but how does it fare with our poor friends at the Crags, who are nobly enduring hunger and cold, and every privation in the cause of our common Lord? My heart bleeds for them; let us therefore instantly send them a portion from our table, that their hearts too may be comforted." To this proposal the worthy family cordially responded, and it was agreed to despatch forthwith a young female servant belonging to the household with what provisions she could carry to the friends in their lonely concealment at the Crags. The young woman whom the family wished to perform for them this deed of beneficence, was in all likelihood selected as a person to whom less suspicion would be attached if she was seized on the way than to one of themselves. She, however, had her own fears, and seemed unwilling to proceed, lest she should encounter the troopers on the moorland, and lest, through her weakness, she should be tempted to reveal her errand, and consequently the haunt of the worthies. William Swan endeavoured to allay her fears by representing to her the guardian care of Providence, and by showing the praiseworthy nature of the deed she was called to perform, assuring her if she was interrupted and interrogated by the enemy that courage and words would be given her both how to behave and how o answer. Being therefore induced to comply, and having mustered all her fortitude for the attempt, she set out laden with provisions. A moor of some extent lay between Braehead and the Crags, over the desert tracks of which she had to pass ere she reached her destination, and it was here mainly that danger was to be dreaded. As she entered on this moorland waste nothing was to be seen calculated to excite alarm, and she proceeded onward in hope of escaping interruption. On a sudden, however, her fond expectations were blasted, for she descried a company of horsemen advancing in the distance, and apparently marching in a straight line to the place where she was. In a few minutes the dragoons stood before her, and in an imperious tone asked her what it was she was carrying, and where she was going. She appeared unwilling to reply; this excited their suspicion, and they affirmed that she was conveying food to the rebels, and expressed their determination to know the whole matter before they parted. In her great perplexity she happened to observe on the neighbouring hill a number of persons casting turf, and she immediately resolved to turn aside to them, hoping that under the pretext of carrying food to the labourers she would escape further annoyance. This new idea inspired her with courage, and she began to address the soldiers with considerable freedom, and asked them to accompany her to the height, where the whole of the secret which they seemed so anxious to know might perhaps be fully unfolded. The people who were employed on the bent were persons whom she did not know; but as she expected more favour from the peasants than from the dragoons, she thought it probable that they would understand the nature of her situation, and receive her as if she were a person well known to them, and that by this means the suspicion of the troopers would be allayed. Her plan was successful, for the soldiers without more ado marched off towards Dalswinton; but not before they received a severe reprimand for their unmannerly interruption. She was now left alone to pursue her way unmolested; and instead of visiting the workmen on the hill, she went straight to the cave, and performed the truly Christian service on which her master had sent her. Her escape prevented, perhaps, the ruin of her master's household, and saved the lives of the worthies in the cave; and was, in all likelihood, a direct answer to the prayers of William Swan, whose care for Christ's suffering people induced him to employ every means for their welfare. A number of years after the termination of the persecution a large Bible was found in the cave, which doubtless had been used by the pious persons who were forced to take refuge there. A leaden pitcher was also discovered, which probably belonged to the hospitable tenant of Braehead. Both the Bible and the pitcher would no doubt be preserved as valuable relics by those into whose possession they came.

Shortly after this, one of the outed ministers having visited the neighbourhood, it was agreed that a conventicle should be held at a place called Wardlaw, at some distance from Braehead. These zealous servants of Christ embraced every opportunity of preaching the gospel, even at the imminent risk of their lives. It was for this end they lived, and in this good work they were ready to die. The visits of such men were occasions of much spiritual refreshment to the people of God, who flocked in great numbers from all parts to hear from their lips the precious words of life. On the day of the meeting a large company assembled from the surrounding district in the expectation of spending one Sabbath in the worship of God without disturbance. There was a person of the name of Smith, who resided within the farm of Braehead, a low, selfish character, who expected to reap some worldly advantage at the expense of the meeting at Wardlaw. After the worship was begun, and when the minister in the tent which was reared in the field, was preaching to the people who were listening with all earnestness to his discourse, Smith, who was watching his opportunity, came running in great haste to the outskirts of the crowd, crying that a company of d.agoons were speedily approaching. This report, which was entirely false, at once threw the multitude into confusion, and occasioned the dispersion of the congregation—the very thing which Smith wanted. In the disorder of the moment, when the people were running to and fro, not knowing which hand to turn to, the temporary tent was overturned with the minister in it, but without any injury to his person, and one man who had tethered his horse in an adjoining field that it might graze at leisure during the service, in his haste and trepidation, vaulted the animal, forgetting to untie the cord by which he was bound, and spurring furiously, both the horse and his rider were nearly, if not actually overturned by the sudden check which the rope, when drawn with violence to its full stretch, occasioned. When the congregation had vacated the spot, and not an individual remained in the field, Smith at his leisure gathered the bonnets and plaids and bibles, and other articles which the people, in the scene of confusion that ensued, had left behind them. Having collected the spoil he returned to his house, ike a person loaded with the plunder of the slain from the field of battle. This man, actuated by a principle of sordid avarice, was guilty of a base falsehood and of a disgraceful theft, and deprived a great company of hearing the gospel on one of those occasions which was but rarely enjoyed in those days of tribulation and hazard. Covetousness is one of the worst of those vile affections which have a place in our depraved nature: it was this which prompted Judas to betray our Lord, and it has caused the ruin of innumerable souls. There are perhaps few vices which lurk more insidiously in the heart than this: for men may be under its reigning power without being aware of it, and no evidence is more decisive against a man's christianity than the dominant love of the world: "Love not the world, neither the things that are in the world; for if any man love the world, the love of the Father is not in him."

After the affair of the conventicle, Smith fell into a state of great mental distress. A sense of the impiety of his conduct in this instance, combined with the conviction of the general irreligiousness of his character in other respects, drove him to distraction. He lived despised by others, and despising himself till his life became an insupportable burden, and, like Judas, he hanged himself. He was found suspended in one of the out-houses belonging to William Swan, by his own sister, and the circumstance created the deepest sensation in the neighbourhood. As soon as the news of the painful occurrence spread abroad, every person seemed horror-struck, for he was regarded as a very wicked man, and his end was viewed as the natural consequence of his nefarious life. This poor man, instead of fleeing to the Saviour for the forgiveness of his sins, yielded to despair, not understanding that all sins, the greatest and the least, alike may be pardoned on the ground of the glorious propitiation of our great High Priest, who "is able to save to the uttermost." Despair of divine mercy originates in a great measure in the powerful legal bias of the unrenewed heart, which prompts us to entertain the supposition, that according to the degree of a man's criminality his pardon is difficult or easy, that God is more ready to forgive a less sin than a greater, and that if we were more worthy, we might with the greater confidence come to him. All this, however, is obviously unsound, for the gospel of the grace of God offers salvation to all men without difference, be their sins many or few, because the infinitely efficacious blood of Christ cleanseth from *all* sin.

In former times, and even till a very recent period, public opinion respecting suicide was peculiar, and so peculiar as to forbid the sepulture in the common burying-ground, of all persons who terminated their lives by their own act. Happily, however, this opinion is, in our times, greatly modified, if not altogether changed. In the days of William Swan, however, the feeling against such persons ran to the highest extreme, and the body of Smith was not allowed interment in the church-yard. In such cases the custom was to bury on neutral land, either on the march between two counties, or between two gentlemen's estates, that the dust of such unhappy persons might not find a resting-place on any claimable property. There is a spot on the Lowther hills, exactly on the borders of Nithsdale and Lanarkshire, which for many generations was employed as a burial-place of the victims of suicide. It was with great difficulty that any individual could be found to remove the body of Smith, and to prepare it for burial; even his own nearest kindred refused to touch him, and he might have remained suspended till the flesh fell from his bones, had not the laird of Dalswinton induced a person to convey the corpse in a car to a place called Auchengeith, on the march between the lairds of Closeburn and Queensbury, where he was buried. This deed of Smith, and his character generally, were so detested, that honest William Swan could not endure even to see the house standing in which he ended his life, and he forthwith demolished it, not leaving one stone upon another, that he might obliterate the scene of so vile an action, and testify his disapprobation of a character so infamous.

"Upon the 8th of May, 1679," says Wodrow, "the council emit a proclamation against travelling with arms without license. It is founded upon the atrocious acts committed by persons who go to field-conventicles, and discharges all subjects to travel with arms without license, and appoints all magistrates to seize such, except noblemen, landed-gentlemen, and their children, and servants in company with them, if they be found with arms, and the soldiers are likewise ordered to apprehend such." After the passing of this act a strict search was made for arms, especially in those parts of the country where the greatest dissatisfaction was known to exist. The terror lest the peasantry would defend themselves in case of aggression, or perhaps execute vengeance on those who oppressed them whenever an opportunity should present itself, dictated, no doubt, this measure. In the general search for arms, then, a party of dragoons visited Braehead for the purpose of securing what warlike implements they might find in the possession of the tenant. William Swan, however, was beforehand with them; for having heard of the act, and knowing the uncompromising rigour with which the search would be made, he carried his arms to the roof of the house and concealed them carefully among the thatch. In this place they were as secure as on the top of a mountain, and the honest man rested satisfied that search would be fruitless. When the soldiers arrived they explored every corner, but found nothing. There was a poor widow who lived on the same farm, whose house also they received orders to search, and to her residence they now proceeded. This woman's husband and his brother had been Covenanters, but at this time were in their graves. They died not by the immediate hand of persecution, but rather in consequence of the hardships to which they were subjected; and thus, though they were not slain with the sword, nor shot with the musket, nor hanged on the gibbet, for their adherence to the cause of truth, still they were truly martyrs, for their death was the result of self-denial, and privation, and suffering for Christ's sake. It was on account, therefore, of the well-known non-conformity of her husband that this poor woman's dwelling was to undergo a search. William Swan knowing that she was a worthy person, and that she preserved the arms of her deceased husband, with a superstitious care, often burnishing them, and then depositing them in a place where they might not receive the slightest tarnish, was solicitous on her account, and requested her to conceal them among the thatch as he had done. To this, however, she would not consent, but determined still to keep them below the bed-clothes, the place where she had hitherto retained them. When the soldiers left Braehead, Swan accompanied them to the widow's house, anxious to witness the result, and ready to intercede in case of a discovery. The widow had that same morning gone to the moss to prepare peats for her winter's fuel, and had locked the door behind her; but previous to her departure, she had made ready a large *cog* of sowens for her children's breakfast, which she had placed below the bed-clothes to keep them warm. Strachan, who is said to have been the commander of the party, without ceremony burst open the door, and entering, immediately commenced the search for the arms under the bed-clothes—a circumstance which proves that he had received due information of the place where he would find them. In his haste to seize the weapons, however, he thrust his hand to the wrist into the scalding sowens, the effect of which, like a sudden and powerful shock of electricity, made him spring back to the middle of the floor, while the warm viscous substance was dripping like clotted blood from his ruddy hand, the pain of which was intolerable. "Run to the brook, Captain Strachan," cried William Swan, who scarcely understood the state of things till the matter was more fully investigated. The affair afforded the soldiers unspeakable merriment, especially when they saw their magnanimous leader rinsing his hand and arm in the cleansing and cooling stream. The circumstance, however, put an end to the search for arms; and William Swan was gratified to think that neither he nor the poor woman was likely to be put to any further trouble for the present.

William Swan of Braehead lived to the great age of ninety-six, and "came to his grave in a full age, like as a shock of corn cometh in his season; an old man and full of years, and was gathered to his people." "The memory of the just shall be blessed;" and the memorial of this good man is still warmly cherished, not only by his descendants, but by all to whom his good report has reached. His daughter, Helen Swan, was seventy-four years old when she was gathered to her fathers; and his grand-daughter, Helen Fraser, who lives in the village of Minihive in Dumfries-shire, is at present seventy-seven.

CHAPTER VII.

Bellybught—Scene at Auchengrouch—The Pursuit.

The farm at Bellybught, in the parish of Morton, is situated in a very wild spot among the mountains, and in the times of our suffering ancestors, was occasionally resorted to as a place of seclusion from the fury of their persecutors. In this wilderness there was a lonely shieling, which stood in a moor encircled with hills, and in its neighbourhood was a deep and rugged ravine, whose precipitous sides were thickly covered with wood, the dark recesses of which afforded a sure and safe retreat. On one occasion, a company of wanderers, one of whom was Adam Clark of Glenim, mentioned in a former chapter, had concealed themselves in this solitary haunt. Adam on several accounts was generally regarded as a leader by the party with whom he was connected, and their movements were usually guided by his direction. In this dreary seclusion, they held delightful communion on spiritual things, and enjoyed much sweet intercourse with God. It was to preserve unimpaired the full liberty of worshipping according to their conscience the God of their fathers, that they withstood the unrighteous usurpation of those who wished to place about their necks the yoke both of a spiritual and a political bondage, and hence they sought, and found, in the remote solitudes that freedom which could not elsewhere be enjoyed. In this exile, however, they were often in much distress through hunger; and unless when a friend who knew their situation brought them a supply, they were obliged to travel to a considerable distance, and in great secrecy, to procure food to preserve their lives. An anecdote is told of a pious man, who had secluded himself in a cave by the water of Ae, and who was so closely watched by his enemies, that he dared not venture abroad night nor day for a considerable time. In this situation, being greatly afflicted with hunger, he observed a large wild fowl that alighted very near the mouth of his cell, and deposited an egg among the heather. This was done every morning, and on this provision he was sustained during the time of his concealment in the cavern; and in this way, as the Lord preserved the life of his prophet by the brook Cherith, when the ravens brought him bread and flesh in the morning, and bread and flesh in the evening, was this good man, who trusted in God, supported. In the one case the supply was miraculous, and in the other not; still the hand of a guardian Providence was as much concerned in the one case as in the other. In ordinary circumstances we are not to expect that the Lord will supply our wants in any other way than in the use of means; and therefore, while we pray, "Give us this day our daily bread," we are at the same time to labour with our hands to earn an honest subsistence; for the exercise of faith and the diligent use of means are to be combined. In those cases, however, in which we are precluded from using means, we are authorized to trust in God, believing that he will supply our wants in one way or in another; for he will sooner rain bread from the clouds, than suffer the confidence of his people to be defeated.

Adam Clark, who was a robust and active young man, and well acquainted with the locality, issued, with one or two of his companions, from their hiding-place in the night season, for the purpose of providing a meal for the rest who remained in the shieling. He obtained his errand, and returned in safety before the early dawn, congratulating himself and his friends on his success. The party, amounting in all to twenty-eight persons, having with grateful hearts participated of the welcome viands which He who provides for the wants of all his creatures had set before them, were reposing securely within the hut, when Clark and his brother Andrew, standing near the door, observed a ewe pass with startling haste, and then another, pursued by a swift and powerful dog. "What means this?" exclaimed Andrew. "It is one of Morton's dogs," replied Adam; "our retreat is discovered, and the troopers will be here instantly." The party within were roused to a sense of their danger, and every man had his defensive weapons in readiness. Scarcely had they accoutred themselves, when the dragoons in thundering haste surrounded the hiding-place. The friends within rushed simultaneously to the bent, for the purpose if possible, of making their escape. The leader of the troopers commanded them to seize Clark, come of the rest what might. He was instantly attacked by a powerful dragoon, and Clark, having caught his horse by the bridle reins, pushed him backwards till he stumbled and overthrew his rider. The dragoon was now fully in his power, but he spared his life; resting contented with having come off victorious, and unscathed in the perilous scuffle. In the meantime his attention was directed to another quarter, where he saw his brother prostrated in a moss, and a gigantic dragoon standing over him, and about to hew him in pieces with his ponderous broadsword. Adam sprang to his assistance, and in a moment was at his side. The dragoon turned round to defend himself from the attack of his new opponent, and left Andrew uninjured. In the conflict Adam wrested the sword from the hand of the soldier, and having thrown him on the heath, descended with his companions into the ravine or deep gullet, formed by the rushing of the mountain torrent, in the bosky recesses of which they found a retreat from the vengeance of their foes, who dared not venture after them, lest they should receive a fatal shot by the party unseen, from the heart of the dark bushes in which they were hid. Thus did Providence defend this little band of Christian patriots; and while it must have been a matter of thankfulness to them, that no one of their number was missing, nor any of them seriously hurt, it must have been no less satisfactory, that they had left none of their enemies dead on the scene of conflict. Their object was not to destroy the lives of others, but to preserve their own; and if at any time in self-defence they took away life, it was not because they had pleasure in it, but because necessity compelled them.

Many years after this, when the Revolution settlement had made foes friends again, Adam Clark, now a peaceful store-farmer among the hills of his native district, happened to be in the city of Edinburgh, to which place he had driven a flock of sheep for sale. As he was strolling along the streets he was accosted by a tall and strongly-built man, who asked him if he did not recognize him. "No," said Clark, "I do not know you; you seem an entire stranger to me." "I know you, however, having once met with you in circumstances which I shall not easily forget." "To what do you allude?" replied Clark. "Do you not remember," said the man, "the onslaught at Bellybught? Do you not remember the dragoon from whom you wrested the sword, and whom you left prostrate in the moss?" "I do," answered Clark, "and are you the man?" "I am; and to you I owe my life, for you had me completely in your power; I am beyond measure happy that I now have the opportunity of rendering to you my cordial thanks for your clemency; and I trust that God, in opposition to whose cause I then fought, has in his graciousness turned my heart to himself. From the moment I escaped from you with my life, I never lifted a weapon on the side of persecution, and I most sincerely regret that I ever enlisted in that cause; but I, like Paul, did it ignorantly and in unbelief." Clark was astonished; he grasped him by the hand, and hailed him as a brother, and rejoiced that, having left the path of the destroyer, he had found the way that leads to peace and everlasting life. "Have you still the sword," asked the reclaimed trooper, "which you twisted so bravely from my grasp?" "I have," replied Clark, "and I intend to keep it as an heir-loom in my family." "Keep it then, you bravely deserve it; and let it never more be employed, but in an honest cause." There is something exceedingly agreeable in an occurrence of this kind. Two men who once met in deadly strife on the battle-field, meeting again in times of peace, and meeting with hearts united in the same bonds of Christian fellowship, attached to the cause of the same common Lord, and sharers of the same common salvation, is indeed a circumstance worthy of notice, and delightfully illustrative of the power of the gospel on the heart.

On another occasion, a company of troopers, who were on their way to the wilds of Crawford moor, for the purpose of surprising a conventicle which was to be held in that solitary retreat, called at Glenim, which lay directly in their route, to ask a guide to conduct them over the heights. When the party drew up before the door, Adam Clark went out to meet them, and in stooping, as the story tells, to draw one of his shoes more firmly on his foot, being newly roused from his bed, as it was in the dark of the morning when the soldiers arrived, he was jostled by one of the horses, and nearly thrown down. In recovering his position, his temper being a little heated, he struck the animal a furious blow on the face, which made him retreat rather hastily and awkwardly for his rider, who instantly presented a pistol to Clark's breast, with the apparent intention of shooting him on the spot. The commander of the party seeing the mischief that might befal, interfered; and presenting the broad side of his sword to the dragoon, prevented him from fulfilling his purpose, declaring that they had come with no hostile intent, but simply to request the assistance of a guide. This occurrence, it is probable, took place prior to the affair at Bellybught, and near the beginning of the persecution, when the sentiments of the Clarks, both of Auchengrouch and Glenim, in reference to public matters, were not generally known. When order was restored, and parties had come to a better understanding, Clark consented to conduct them across the wilds. When they came to a place on the west side of the Lowther hills, not far from the mining village of Wanlockhead, called the Stake moss, it occurred to Clark that now it was in his power to occasion them some inconvenience, which might probably retard their progress, and prevent them from accomplishing their intended mischief. This moss presents an irregular surface, with here and there deep hags, and some marshy springs. These springs, or cold wells as the shepherds term them, are some of them in the moorland districts in the south-west of Scotland, of great depth, reaching occasionally from six to twelve feet, and in some cases to a much greater depth. Their breadth is sometimes found to be about two or three feet, and their length more than double. The water in these wells rises to a level with the surrrounding heath, and its surface is generally covered with long grass and aquatic weeds. A dragoon on horseback stumbling into one of these larger wells, the ordinary springs being much less in dimensions and in depth, would inevitably perish; and this amply accounts for the tradition respecting the occasional and entire disappearance of some of the troopers, man and horse, in the moors. It was in the dusk of the early morning when the party arrived at the Stake moss, and the obscurity was favourable to Clark's design. They had followed him in safety for several miles; and, having no suspicion of their guide, they rode behind him in perfect confidence. At length, having reached the morass, Clark, being on foot, pressed forward, leaping the mossy ditches with a nimble bound; and the horses plunging after, one after another stuck fast in the sinking peat ground. When Clark saw that the party were fully bemired, and that there was little chance of their getting themselves extricated for a considerable time, he made his escape over the dark heath, and left them to help themselves. It is said that he often regretted his conduct on this occasion; both because he deemed it treacherous, seeing the commander of the party treated him honourably, and because it would tend to exasperate the enemy, and subject all the friends throughout the district to a still more rigorous treatment; and his suspicions were not groundless. The more injury the Covenanters, in self-defence, inflicted on their opponents, the more severe did their own sufferings afterwards become; for their enemies delighted in nothing more than in an opportunity of retaliating with sevenfold vengeance. It appears that Adam Clark, from the time that he led the troopers into the moss, was regarded as a dangerous man, and one whom, on the first opportunity, they were determined to apprehend. This determination was amply manifested in the tragic scene which had well nigh been fully acted on the bent before the house of Auchengrouch. It seems that young Andrew Clark of Auchengrouch bore a striking resemblance to his cousin, Adam of Glenim. One day the dragoons met Andrew on the moors, and believing him to be the identical person who guided them into the moss, apprehended him, and carried him to his father's house. The commander of the party is said to have been Colonel James Douglas, to whom, as Wodrow informs us, an ample commission, with a justiciary power, was granted, for the purpose of harassing the west and south. The poor captive was interrogated respecting his principles, and especially in reference to his conduct at the moss. He declared that he was not the person to whom he alluded, and that, however strong a resemblance there might be between him and the individual who had done them the injury of which they complained, he was entirely innocent. The soldiers, however, positively affirmed that he was the very man who, in the grey of the morning, conducted them along the heights, and left them in the morass, where they sustained no small damage—having, as they asserted, lost some of their best horses, whose legs were broken in the moss. In those days the execution of a man after nis impeachment was but the work of a moment; and Andrew was immediately brought out to the field before the house to be instantly shot. He was allowed time to pray—a favour which, in similar circumstances, was not granted to every one. He knelt down on the grass, and, in the presence of his enemies and of all his father's household, in the presence of angels and before Him for whose truth he was now bearing testimony, and ready to seal that testimony with his blood, he prayed. In the immediate prospect of death, he poured out his soul before the Lord, and made supplication to his Judge. With a melting heart, and in the confidence of faith, he sought acceptance through the great Intercessor, and the remission of all his iniquities through that precious blood which was shed for the sins of the world. He prayed for support in this trying hour; and besought that as God had brought him to witness publicly for his truth, he would now comfort his heart with the joy of that truth, and enable him to triumph over the fear of death, and submissively, if not exultingly, to surrender his life at Christ's call. Nor would supplication for his enemies, who were now going to deprive him of life, and for his beloved kindred, from whose dear embraces he was now about to be torn, be omitted. The supplications of this good man, like the powerful and subduing prayer of that great Christian, John Brown, of Priesthill, produced a deep impression on the dragoons, who stood around guarding the suppliant as he rested in the attitude of prayer on the heath; and one of the party, more hardened than the rest, perceiving the effect, commanded him to rise from his knees. "No," said the leader, "let the poor man continue in his prayer, we can afford to wait a little; other matters are not pressing; give the man leisure, as his time on earth is but short." There are few hearts so indurated as fairly to outbrave a scene of this nature without some emotion; and James Douglas, though he had witnessed many an act of cruelty, was, in the present instance, scarcely proof against the moving spectacle of a fellow-creature uttering his last prayer, in the presence of weeping and agonizing friends; and, probably, he now wanted only a slight pretext to set the poor victim free, and that pretext was soon found. There lived in the neighbourhood, at a place called Howat's-burn-foot, an aged and worthy woman, who had been Andrew Clark's nurse, and for whom, as is common in such cases, she cherished a more than ordinary affection. To this good woman's hut a messenger was instantly despatched to convey the information of what was going on at Auchengrouch. She was a woman of great sagacity, and magnanimity, and piety, who had seen much, both in her native country and in foreign lands; for she had accompanied her husband for sixteen years in the continental wars, and had experienced a variety of fortune. On one occasion, it is said, at the storming of a certain town, when her husband had received a severe wound, she first having rendered him on the spot what assistance was necessary, next, in order to supply his lack of service, grasped his sword, and pressed forward with the assailants to the attack. Her name, a circumstance to be regretted, has not been preserved; but her worthy character and disinterested actions have found a place in the memory of posterity. This woman lost no time in presenting herself before Colonel Douglas and his company. The sight of soldiers, even in their most terrific array, did not frighten her, for she had been familiar with war. When she arrived at the scene of distress, Andrew had ended his prayer; and the soldiers were prepared, and waiting their commander's orders, to pour the contents of their muskets into the body of the unoffending victim. "Halt, soldiers," cried the matron, whose venerable and commanding aspect inspired the party with something like awe: "halt, soldiers," cried she, elevating her staff in the attitude of authority, as generals are accustomed to do with the naked blade of their swords on the battle-field, "halt, and listen to me. Let not the brown heath on the moors of Auchengrouch be stained with the blood of an innocent man, lest it cry for vengeance in a voice so loud, and so importunate, as not to be denied." "How now, good mother," said Douglas, "what have you to offer in exculpation of this rebel, who has done what he could to endamage his majesty's interests? You have heard of the affair of the Stake moss?" "I have; but hear me, this man is not he whom you have to blame for that project: he may be like him, he may be his very picture, but he is not the same. Who *he* is that did that deed, it does not befit me to tell, nor shall I. But, sir, if you be a true soldier, hearken to the wife of one who warred under the banner of your honoured uncle in countries far from this; and, for your uncle's sake, by whose side my husband fought and bled, and for whose sake he would have sacrificed his life, I beg the life of this man, for whom, in his infancy, I acted the part of a mother, and for whom, now in his prime of manhood, I cherish all the warmth of a mother's true affection. I beg on my knees the life of this innocent man." "My good woman," replied the Colonel, "his life you shall have. Your appearance is the guaranty for the verity of your statements, and you have mentioned a name that has weight with me. Soldiers! let him go!"

In this way was the tragical scene at Auchengrouch terminated, and Andrew Clark restored to the arms of his rejoicing friends. Many a blessing would doubtless be poured on the head of the worthy matron by whose intercession his life was spared; and she had her reward in the satisfaction of seeing the life of the guiltless prolonged, and in the consciousness that she had performed a worthy action. There is in goodness, combined with true greatness of mind, a dignity which, when witnessed even in the humblest walks of life, commands respect, and overawes those whose station in life is much superior. How great a blessing must such "a mother in Israel" prove to a whole neighbourhood! She is like a centre from which emanate goodness, and wisdom, and experience; and the influence of her prudent and godly example must tell with great efficiency on the entire circle of her acquaintanceship. Such a woman is a crown to her husband, an honour to her kindred, and an ornament to the gospel of Christ. The circumstances also in which Andrew Clark was placed brought his Christian character fairly and fully to the test; he was made to look death in the face, and all the realities of eternity were near, but he continued steadfast, and was ready to part with his life for Christ's sake.

Another anecdote is told of two honest men, who, in this same locality, experienced a deliverance from the hands of their persecutors, similar to that which Andrew Clark experienced at Auchengrouch. A covenanter, whose name is not known, had been caught by his enemies, and, under the conduct of two dragoons from Elliock or from Sanquhar, was conveyed through the mountains to be delivered to the custody of a garrison, somewhere on the Clyde. As the dragoons were moving slowly along with their solitary charge, they observed in the neighbourhood of Thristane, a place not far from Glenim, a man on the opposite hill clad in a red jacket. "Yonder," exclaimed one of the troopers, "yonder is our deserter; guard the prisoner, and I will pursue." The shepherd on the height observed the movement, and, seeing the dragoon advancing with all haste, fled. This circumstance was enough to confirm the suspicions of the soldier, who quickened his pace, thinking him a prize worth the seizing. The shepherd, whose name was Harper, sped his way along the slope of the hill, and took refuge in his own house. When he entered his dwelling he hastily doffed his red vest, justly suspecting that it was the cause of the pursuit, and hid it under the bed-clothes. The dragoon followed, and entered the house in breathless haste, thinking that now he was sure of his prey. "Where is the man," demanded he, "where is the man with the red jacket? Deliver him instantly, he is a deserter from our party; and our orders are to apprehend him, and bring him to punishment. I demand him in the king's name." Harper, who was now arrayed in the ordinary garb of a shepherd, and was sitting with apparent composure by the fire, with a child on his knee, replied that there was no person in his house wearing a dress such as was described. "I saw him enter," vociferated the dragoon, "and he must be here." "You are at liberty to search every corner of this house," said Harper, "and if you find him, you shall be welcome to hold him your prisoner." The trooper, after an unsuccessful search, and after having, as was customary in such cases, stabbed the bed with his sword, departed without his object. When he was gone, the jacket was drawn from the bed perforated in many places by the point of the sharp weapon, but it was never again used as an article of clothing. During the time that the zealous dragoon was searching the house of Thristane, his fellow-soldier was halting with his prisoner till his return. The place where they stood, was on the edge of a precipitous brow, which descended to a great depth into the valley beneath. The Covenanter, whose arms were firmly bound together at the wrists like an infamous felon, thought, that now, if he were unbound, he might easily make his escape. With this idea, he requested the soldier to untie his hands for a few minutes, giving as a reason for this request what satisfied the dragoon. Having obtained his desire, he seated himself on the grass on the very brink of the descent, and while his guard paid no attention to his movements, he seized his limbs by the ancles, and bending his head forward, threw his body into something like the shape of a wheel, and tumbled with great velocity down the steep, and then starting to his feet fled at his utmost speed. The dragoon, taken by surprise, was confounded at the incident, and, hastily grasping his musket, fired, but without success, as it is always difficult to secure an effective aim with fire-arms in a sloping direction. He was instantly joined by the trooper from Thristane, and the two commenced a vigorous pursuit. The fugitive, however, fled with great speed, and escaped to the wilds near the source of the Clyde, where he found a shelter from his deadly foes; the God in whom he trusted having accomplished his deliverance.

CHAPTER VIII.

Muirkirk—John Richard—Thomas Richard—William Moffat of Hartfell.

The farm-house of Burnfoot, in times of persecution, stood on the moorland stream of Greenock water, at a short distance from the village of Muirkirk, around which on the wilds and mountains many a deed of persecuting cruelty was perpetrated. It was in the neighbourhood of this village that John Brown, of Priesthill, a man whose saintly character earned for him the epithet of the *godly carrier*, fell by the murderous hand of Claverhouse, on the green turf before his own door. The solitudes in the vicinity of Muirkirk were frequently crowded with the scattered flock of Christ, when they were driven with the rod of violence from those pastures on which they had been formerly nurtured. Muirkirk, which is now a large and crowded village, was in those more simple times a small hamlet with its little church sitting solitary afar on the waste; but even here, in the lonely wilderness, was the gospel of our salvation faithfully preached to the handful of the rural population that weekly convened in the house of God. The name of Hugh Campbell, the minister of the parish, is to be found on the roll of the ejected. This circumstance speaks for his faithfulness as a servant of Christ, and would authorize us to draw the inference that he was one of those who maintained the standard of the truth, when Zion's foes were striving to wrest it from the hands of her children. The dreary locality in the midst of which Muirkirk is situated, must have afforded, for a considerable period, a place of refuge to those who were driven before the storm, and buffetted by the fierce blasts of a relentless persecution. At length every retreat, however remote, was carefully searched by those whose delight it was to drive the plough share of ruin through a prostrate land; and the wilds of Muirkirk afforded a spacious hunting field to those whose occupation it was to shed on the flowery heath, without a tear, the blood of God's saints. The deep mossy trenches on the moun tain's side were often made to flow with the blood of those who, for the truth's sake, jeoparded their lives on the high places of the field, and whose death-groans were heard to mingle with the soft wailings of the gentle lambkins on the moors; but in the absence of all human condolence, we can believe that the consolations of the Holy Spirit were not wanting, and that the sweet accents of music uttered, it may be, by the blessed lips of angels or of sister spirits, whose martyred bodies were sleeping in the neighbouring heath, soothed their dying moments, and fortified their hearts in the parting hour. There is, in the desert "flowered with martyrs," presented to the eye of the Christian, a beauty, compared with which the finest and richest scenes on earth are tame and bleak. There is felt by the devout heart a moral interest in the scenery, which stirs all the inner soul, and which binds to the spot his holiest likings.

John Richard, the occupant of the farm of Burnfoot, was a Covenanter. Irvine of Bonshaw, who was at this time ravaging the west, proceeded with a few dragoons, to Burnfoot, for the purpose of apprehending the worthy tenant. In order the better to accomplish his purpose, he resolved to adopt the night season, when the quiet family would be gathered about the blazing hearth. The night selected for the work of mischief happened to be extremely dark; and this circumstance gave rise to a proverbial expression, which was long current in the district. When any evening was more than commonly *murky*, it was said to be "like Bonshaw's night." The obscurity of the night, however, was the safety of the family at Burnfoot. There happened to be in Bonshaw's party a dragoon of the name of McLelland, who was formerly a servant to John Richards; and this individual, though a wild and reckless character, entertained a respect for the household in which he had once resided, and availing himself of the pitchy darkness of the evening, he stole from his company, and being well acquainted with the locality, proceeded unobserved, and with all speed, to the house of his old master. The family were out of measure astonished when they saw McLelland coming swaggering into the apartment, in the attire of a rough dragoon. In his vapouring manner he explained the object of his visit; and having drawn his ponderous blade, struck the *crook* or pendant chain in the chimney thrice, leaving each time a deep notch in the iron, by which he said Tom McLelland would be kept in memory when his bones were in the dust. The rude kindness of the blunt dragoon was not unappreciated by the honest farmer of Burnfoot and his family, who instantly prepared for flight. McLelland returned to his party and joined them, without having been missed, or in any way suspected. As they approached the house, McLelland was loudest in his denunciations of vengeance against the whigs. The party alighted on a gentle rising ground, on which was reared a huge pyramid of peats, and prepared to make their attack on the defenceless dwelling. Bonshaw then rushed into the house, expecting to seize its inmates by surprise; but, to his astonishment, nobody was within. The search which followed was fruitless, and the object of the troopers was unexpectedly defeated. John Richards being an aged man, and not able to retire far from his house in the dark, had cowered down at the side of a stone dyke in the close vicinity of his cottage. The feet of the horses, in moving about in the dark, had nearly trodden upon

10

him. Perceiving his danger, he, with as little noise and with as much haste as he could, removed from the spot, and crept on the wet ground into the midst of some willow bushes that grew near the place. As he lay here, the horses accidentally approached him again; and he was not without the serious apprehension of being crushed to death under their feet. The boggy ground, however, saved him; for the heavy animals sank to the belly in the marsh, and with difficulty were extricated. The dragoons finding themselves thus incommoded, and seeing that their object could not be gained at the time, withdrew. Bonshaw, notwithstanding the bewildering darkness of the night, was yet resolved to make further attempts in another place that lay in his route. Not far from Burnfoot they stumbled on a weaver's hut, into which they entered, for the purpose of making inquiries, and of procuring a guide. The weaver had just returned from the house of one of his customers to whom he had carried a newly-wrought web; and being dressed in his better clothes, the leader of the party asserted that he had been at a conventicle, or some private meeting of the Covenanters, and that therefore he must be a whig. The man endeavoured to clear himself of the charges, and showed them the true state of the matter. Bonshaw then declared his readiness to believe him on the following conditions—that he should swear never to lift arms against the king, and that he should conduct them to the farm-house of Netherwood. The weaver, being no Covenanter, consented to do both. When the party reached Netherwood, the leader succeeded in obtaining another guide to conduct them to Greenock-mains, at which he expected to apprehend some of the Covenanters. The guide from

Netherwood appears to have been the farmer him self, and had no great liking for the business on which he was pressed. He found it in vain to remonstrate, but resolved, if possible, to make the errand of the troopers to Greenock Mains abortive. Near the house of Greenock Mains is a steep brow, down the descent of which Netherwood led the company. It was this honest man's design to convey, by some means or other, a warning to the family of Greenock Mains, of the danger that was approaching. Accordingly, when the party reached the top of the brow, Netherwood, in a pretty loud voice, apprized them of the circumstance, and showed the necessity of using great caution in the descent. As they proceeded almost blindfolded down the declivity, every little incident or stumbling among the horses or men afforded an occasion to Netherwood to lift his voice still louder, by way of caution to the troopers, on the one hand, and by way of warning to the unsuspecting family, on the other. He seemed to be particularly solicitous about the safety of the commander, whose name he took pleasure in vociferating with great emphasis, and giving him incessantly the high-sounding title of "Your Honour," enjoined him to advance warily in the dark, as life and limbs were both in hazard. Bonshaw, apprehensive lest the noise should alarm the inmates of Greenock Mains, imposed silence; but Netherwood, not appearing to apprehend the import of Bonshaw's advice, seemed intent only on the safety of the party intrusted to his guidance, and cried the louder as he approached the dwelling. Bonshaw threatened—

"But Netherwood him *honoured* still,
Till Greenock Mains sped to the hill."

The result was as Netherwood intended, and as

Bonshaw feared; for Greenock Mains fled in the dark, and escaped the hands of his enemies, who thirsted for his blood.

The farmer of Greenock Mains, however, did not always thus escape. The very same person, in all likelihood, of whom the worthless Bonshaw was at this time in quest, was afterwards apprehended and shot at Cumnock: his name was Thomas Richard. Tradition mentions that a Covenanter of the name of Richard was in concealment on the heights between Burnfoot and Evan Water, and that he was apprehended by stratagem. The plan taken to circumvent him was the following: A number of individuals in the guise of Covenanters came upon him in his hiding-place. They pretended to be very serious persons—each had a Bible; and they requested Richard to read the Scriptures with them, and to pray. The good man, suspecting no deceit, rejoiced to meet with a number of religious friends whom he had never seen before, and gladly complied with their request As the sky sometimes assumes a very serene and beautiful aspect immediately before the gathering of the storm, so these men assumed a devout and friendly demeanour, which was soon to issue in that of deceivers and murderers. To the blank astonishment of the simple-minded Covenanter, he soon found that he was their prisoner; and that, instead of their being devout worshippers, they were ruthless persecutors. He was carried to Cumnock, where he suffered martyrdom. This anecdote, with some circumstantial variations, is substantially the same with the account of Thomas Richard of Greenock Mains, given by Wodrow. About this time," says the historian, "a very barbarous murder was committed upon Thomas Richard in Greenock

Mains, in the parish of Muirkirk, a godly man, nearly eighty years of age. Peter Inglis, cornet, son to Captain Inglis, with some soldiers, pretended they were friends, and some of the remains of Argyle's men. One of my informations bears, that, the better way to carry on the cheat, they had Bibles with them, and pressed and prevailed with Thomas to pray with them; and when at prayer, some of them took notes of some expressions, and afterwards they advised with him upon a designed attack they were about to make upon a neighbouring garrison. Two other narratives before me omit these circumstances, and say, Captain Inglis came into Thomas's house with four or five men pretending to be whigs; and, after some other discourse, asked him if he knew where any of the honest party were. The old man, in the innocence of his heart, suspecting no cheat, answered, he knew not of any at present; but that he had lodged some of them some days ago, and was not yet unwilling to give them any entertainment he had. Thus the jest was carried on for a little, till one of them bewrayed himself by an oath, and then they all cast off the mask, and carried the old man to Colonel Douglas, then at Cumnock, who precisely, upon this alleged confession, without jury or trial, next day executed him there. I am well informed, from a reverend minister present, that his case was so favourable, that three ladies of the Episcopal persuasion, upon hearing of it, went to the Colonel to beg his life, but were not admitted, only they had a message sent them "that he could show no favour to these people." The anecdote, and the statement of the historian, seem therefore to be the same. This venerable saint, like many of his brethren in that treacherous age, lost his life in a cruel and iniquitous manner. It is a pity that nothing but the mere incident of his death has been recorded: it would have been gratifying to know the behaviour of this Christian on the eve of martyrdom. But though nothing respecting this has been handed down to us, there is no doubt but that He in whose cause he was called out to suffer before many witnesses, would be with him to strengthen him to bear honourable testimony to the truth.

Having viewed, then, these scenes and doings in the west, we may now turn round, and for a moment glance at some things which were done in an easterly direction. There lived, says tradition, a man of the name of William Moffat, near Hartfell, not far from the beautiful village of Moffat in Annandale. This man, having experienced the power of the truth in his own heart, was solicitous, it would appear, to impart the knowledge of the same truth to others. For this purpose he formed little conventicles among the hills, and prayed with, and instructed those who resorted to him. The wild locality, in the midst of which Providence had fixed his abode, was favourable to the object he had in view, inasmuch as there was less danger of meeting with interruption. Secluded however as this situation was, it was not too secluded from the flying parties of troopers who occasionally scoured moss and mountain in all directions and at all seasons. One day William Moffat had met with a few friends in a retired glen in the vicinity of his dwelling, and was employed with them in religious exercises. While they were engaged in devotion, the large flock of sheep that was quietly grazing on the dark slanting brow of the neighbouring height, was on a sudden observed to be in motion, and then to spread on all sides as if furiously attacked by a pack of ravenous dogs. "We are in danger," cried the honest shepherd, "these sheep are not scattered without a cause." And they were in danger: for a company of dragoons were descending the hill, and the terrified sheep had fled before them, and fled as if to announce to the little flock of worshippers, who were as helpless as themselves, that the enemy was approaching. Whether the troopers were incidentally passing, or had come to make special search, is not said, but they were descending straight on the timid handful who had met in the desert to pray. What was to be done? They could neither fight nor flee, and must therefore inevitably fall a prey to the destroyer. It sometimes happens, however, that when, in certain perilous circumstances, all hope appears to be cut off, even then, in our very extremity, a deliverance unexpectedly comes, and so was it with the worshippers in the glen. Those who are acquainted with the mountainous tracts of the country, are no strangers to the sudden falling of the mist on the summits of the lofty heights. Sometimes, instead of descending in a body like a large snowy cloud spreading itself along the ridges and adown the slopes of the hills, it comes edgewise trailing along, and, like a thin white veil, extending from the clouds to the earth. On the present occasion the vapour that had been encircling the brow of the mountain, and occasionally stretching out in long defiles into the narrow glens beneath, came like a lofty and impervious wall between the worshippers and the dragoons. This covering, which was thus thrown from the clouds, screened from the view of the soldiers the little conventicle, and they marched past beyond the misty curtain, not more, it is said, than a hundred and fifty yards distant. Thus did this small flock of God's worshippers, that had convened in the wilderness to gather the manna that might be rained from his hand, experience his special care, and were protected by him behind a wall of secure defence, when the foe, like the rushing of the tempest, swept past them on the other side. We may easily conceive the grateful emotions that must have stirred within them when they thought on the kindness that shielded them from so great a danger. It is said that this and similar deliverances emboldened the shepherd and his friends to persist in holding frequent meetings for spiritual edification, notwithstanding the hazards to which they were exposed. Their confidence in God's providential care was greatly strengthened when, in answer to prayer, they found protection.

On another occasion William Moffat was surprised by the dragoons, and narrowly escaped twice on the same day. He fled toward Evan Water to hide himself in its woods, or in some friendly house whose door might perchance be open to receive him. In his flight he passed near a place called Raecleuch, and in crossing a streamlet in the view of the house he observed a hollow place close by the margin of the brook, in which, like Peden in Glendyne, he resolved to conceal himself. The dragoons came onward and passed the stream without perceiving him, and pursued their course along the track that led up the Evan. The farmer of Raecleuch had observed the pursuit, and saw Moffat hide himself in the hollow among the bushes by the burn; and when the troopers were passed, and the fugitive had crept from his hiding-place, the honest farmer congratulated him on his escape. The soldiers, however, perceiving that they had missed their object, and standing still to look around them, observed Moffat and the gudeman of Raecleuch conversing together. They instantly retraced their steps, and commenced the pursuit. Moffat perceiving the movement of the horsemen, again betook himself to flight; and having passed the Evan, hied to the heights in the direction of Elvanfoot, in the neighbourhood of which lived a friend of his own, in whose house he hoped to find shelter. With this intention he proceeded onward, and far outstripped the troopers, who could not wend their way through moss and moor with the same celerity and safety. When he came near Elvanfoot he hid himself in the hollow places among the dark heather on the waste, and finally eluded the search of his pursuers. The brown heath was to him doubtless a sweet and soft bed, after the long and perilous chase. The feeling of safety is never so delightfully intense as immediately after escape from imminent danger, nor does the heart ever swell with warmer emotions of grateful acknowledgments to the Preserver of our life. And happy must he have been when, prostrate in concealment and prayer on the bent, he poured out his heart into the "bosom of his Father and his God." The upland solitudes, near the source of the Clyde, in the vicinity of the ancient Roman station at Gadenica, the long sought for town of the Damnii, were much frequented in the times of the church's tribulation, and many a houseless wanderer, for conscience sake, sought here an asylum from the fury of the oppressor.

CHAPTER IX.

Durisdeer—Elias Wilson—Adam Clark, of Glenim—Muncie the informer—Mitchelslacks—Michael Smith, of Quarrel Wood.

THE parish of Durisdeer, in Nithsdale, has already been noticed as the scene of Christian martyrdom, and as occupying a very romantic locality. The name signifies the door of the forest, and plainly indicates, what was the fact, that in ancient times it was mostly covered with wood. The hills, by which it is walled in on the east and on the north, present a scene of indescribable beauty; and in walking along the margin of the Carron, towards the far-famed pass of Dalveen, in the balmy softness of a summer's eve, one would almost imagine that he was transported to the enchanting scenes of the fabled fairy land. This parish is not without its antiquities, and antiquities, too, of considerable interest. On the farm of Castlehill there stood an old baronial stronghold, the residence, no doubt, of some renowned chieftain, whose name and exploits have long since been forgotten; and the fields which were anciently the battle ground of rival clans, are now subjected to the peaceful hand of agriculture. In this locality are the remains of an ancient Roman station, near the church of Durisdeer, and a branch of the Roman road, which went off to the west, and passed through this parish. "This road," says the author of the Caledonia, "went up Nithsdale, on the east side of the Nith, passing by the village of Thornhill, and crossing Carron Water, a little above its influx into the Nith. From this passage the road continued its course, in a northerly direction, past a Roman fort, in a remarkable pass above the kirk of Durisdeer: from this pass it pushed through the hill by the defile called the Wall path, and went down the east side of Powtrail Water, to its confluence with the Dair." It is interesting to think, that in the days of Lollius Urbicus, above seventeen centuries ago, and for ages after, a detachment of Roman soldiers was located in the forest of Durisdeer, speaking the Latin language, and keeping in subjection to the power of Rome the ancient Selgovae, who occupied the upper part of Nithsdale.

Alexander Strang was minister of Durisdeer at the Restoration, and was one of those worthy men who, because he would not submit to lordly prelacy, was banished from his charge. This good man, along with Thomas Shiels, minister of the neighbouring parish of Kirkbride, took joyfully the spoiling of his goods, that he might maintain the doctrine of Christ, and a pure conscience. It is to be regretted, that so little is preserved of those pious men who, for their non-conformity, were ejected by hundreds from their churches, by the unrighteous edicts of unprincipled rulers. Their remembrance, however, is with God, and their labours and their sufferings have long since terminated in the heavenly rest. In more recent times, this upland parish was blessed with the ministrations of an eminently godly man, of the name of McKill. The memory of this heavenly man is still warmly cherished by the older people who in their youth were under his pastoral care. His great diligence in his ministerial labours, his homely and affectionate manners, his fervent and unctuous preaching, and the great gatherings on sacramenta.

occasions, are still spoken of with rapture by the worthy inhabitants of the district. There is a fragrance in piety which embalms the memorial of holy men, and which, like odours wafted afar on the breeze, accompanies their names even to a distant posterity. Godly men, even in obscure stations, are held in grateful remembrance, while heroes and statesmen, and men of great earthly renown in their day, are in a short time forgotten.

There lived in a cottage, on the farm of Dalveen, in the parish of Durisdeer, a Covenanter of the name of Elias Wilson. This man, though occupying the humbler walks of life, was noted for his piety and honesty of principle, and was therefore an individual who could not long be concealed from the observant eye of the persecutors. He was one day informed, that being regarded with suspicion, his enemies at some distance were on their way to apprehend him. He communicated the news to his wife, who was a person in all respects of a kindred spirit with himself, and equally ready to suffer with him in the cause of righteousness and truth. They arranged the affairs of their little dwelling the best way they could, knowing that the unprincipled soldiery would seize every thing they could lay their hands on; and having driven their cow to the bent, they departed, with their infant child, to seek a hiding-place in some lonely cave among the mountains. The cave, in which they found a refuge, was in one of the dark lins of Enterkin, the entrance to which was very difficult and dangerous. The dragoons, as was anticipated, arrived at the cottage at a time when they hoped to capture its inhabitants without much trouble to themselves. In the hut, however, they found matters in a very different situation from what they expected, and being defeated in their object, they were greatly enraged. The cavern, it would appear, to which Wilson and his wife had fled for refuge, was not unknown to some of the dragoons, who proposed to search it, and for this purpose conducted the party to the rocky precipice, in the face of which the dark recess was situated. The approach of the soldiers was perceived by the fugitives, and Wilson accoutred himself for defence. He had brought with him a musket, and with this he was prepared to face his enemies in case of attack. The passage to the hiding place being precarious, the troopers did not seem much inclined to force an entrance, but having posted themselves on all sides, they were determined to annoy the inmates by shooting over the rock and into the mouth of the cave. The manly spirit of Wilson was roused, and the strong affection of the husband and the parent took possession of his whole soul, and urged him fearlessly forward in the defence of his wife and child, against a band of armed ruffians and legalized murderers, whom the spirit of evil had let loose on an unoffending peasantry. A dragoon, more audacious than the rest, had approached near the mouth of the retreat, and leaning over a rock, was peeping into the cave for the purpose of taking his aim at those who were within. This was observed by Wilson, who instinctively stood on the defensive, and fired on the hostile intruder. The shot reached its victim, and the man tumbled from his station into the deep bottom of the ravine below. The commander of the party, who is said to have been a captain Grier, when he saw the man fall by the firing which for a moment illuminated the dark interior of the cavern, was transported with rage, and, breathing a fearful oath, threatened ample vengeance on the detestable Covenanter who, in endeavouring to defend himself, had killed one of the king's troopers. In uttering this threat, however, he reckoned without his host, and forgot that, in certain favourable circumstances, one man is as good as ten. The captain, then, with two of the most daring of his followers, attempted to scramble to the mouth of the cave. Wilson observed their movements, and perceived their dreadful determination; his life was in the utmost jeopardy, and a firm and vigorous defence was now imperatively called for. The assailants had reached the entrance, and were about to rush forward with deadly intent, when Wilson firing again, shot a dragoon, who, staggering backwards, fell against his commander, and both were precipitated into the rocky deep beneath; the soldier was killed by the shot, and the officer by the fall. The remainder of the troopers were astonished and appalled by the catastrophe, and not daring to make a second attempt, resolved to keep watch during the night, while one of their party was despatched to the nearest garrison for assistance. Wilson and his wife now plainly saw that, unless they could steal from their hiding-place, their fate would be inevitable. In making their escape, however, a two-fold difficulty lay in their way—the dangerous passage from the cave in the dark, and the watchfulness of the soldiers who were stationed around them. They resolved, however, to make the attempt, and accordingly, during the midnight vigils of the dragoons, Wilson and his wife softly and unobserved, crept from their prison-house, and left the soldiers in the morning light to wonder at the daring and the dexterity by which their watchfulness had been evaded.

The couple, however, got safe away, and sought another hiding-place, where they were sheltered from the vengeance of their enemies. Wilson was obliged for many a day to keep himself in close concealment, and he succeeded in weathering the storm, and lived to see the Revolution. Providence brought him through many trials, and in the end he died in peace.

It was probably in the same cave to which Wilson and his wife fled, that Adam Clark of Glenim, and a company with him took refuge when they were pursued by the enemy. There lived in Durisdeer a person of the name of Muncie, who bore the character of an infamous informer, and who was constantly prowling about collecting what information he could regarding the wanderers. By some means or other he found out that Clark and his party were lodged in the cavern, and he hastened to make the discovery to those who were in search of them. The dragoons were instantly in motion, and proceeded with all caution to surprise the fugitives in their place of retreat. It happened however, that one of the party in concealment observed from the mouth of the cave, where he chanced to be standing at the moment, the approach of the horsemen; and from the direction in which they were coming, there could be no doubt that they were advancing to assail the hiding-place. It was agreed that, instead of standing a siege in the cavity of the rock, they should betake themselves to flight, and seek their safety on the steep sides of the mountains. They issued without delay from the cavern, and as they were scrambling up the ragged face of the acclivity, the troopers came up and fired upon the fugitives, who were in no condition to defend themselves. One of their number was killed, and the rest escaped to the hills. The name of the person who fell is not known, and his dust is doubtless reposing under the grassy turf on the mountain's side, though no one can point out his resting-place. There are probably scores of our Scottish martyrs, whose graves on the heath, and on the hills, are now entirely unknown. No history has preserved the account of their death, and the narratives which for a season hung on the lips of tradition have now dropt into oblivion.

It was understood by Adam Clark and his party, that Muncie, the informer, was the individual who directed the dragoons to the cavern, and who, consequently, was the cause of the death of their friend; and they determined to embrace the first opportunity of administering a suitable chastisement. They accordingly went in a body to Muncie's house one evening, and found him sitting by the fire, with one of his children on his knee. When they entered, he suspected their errand, and instinctively holding up the child as a sort of shield between himself and his visiters, as if he anticipated an immediate assault, requested them in a fawning and obsequious manner to be seated, and to take supper with him. This they refused in a manner which plainly indicated the design of their visit. Muncie fled to the door—the assailants pursued, and with their hands and other weapons, belaboured him in a style befitting his offence, and expressive of their detestation of his infamous vocation. When the party were engaged in punishing the informer, it is said that a person of the name of the black McMichael struck him with his sword, either accidentally or by design, and killed him. "Evil shall hunt the violent man to over

.hrow him." The retributions of Divine Providence are sometimes very remarkable, and come with such a precision and distinction on their object, as to point him out with full prominence to the notice of all. A man of Muncie's occupation was detested by all parties, and could never enjoy the approbation of his own mind.

On another occasion, this same Adam Clark, and one of his companions, met with rather a remarkable deliverance, under the very eye of Claverhouse and a company of his troops. Clark and his associate, it is said, came in their wanderings to the house of Mitchelslacks, in Closeburn, where they were kindly entertained by the family. Claverhouse, who was then in the neighbourhood, was informed of the circumstance, and proceeded with a party of dragoons to the place. When he arrived at the house, he asked if two men of the description which he gave were within. The mistress of the house, who met him at the door, and who saw that it was in vain to attempt concealment, acknowledged that there were at the time two men such as he had mentioned in the dwelling, and that they were at the moment partaking of some food. "Tell them," said the commander, "to come out instantly: they are our prisoners." The men within, hearing what was going on at the door, rose from the table, and hastily girded on their armour to meet their foes at the entrance. Having loaded their muskets, they presented themselves before the dragoons, prepared for a desperate defence. The bold and martial attitude of the two Covenanters, when they showed themselves in the door-way, overawed the soldiers, ten in number, with Claverhouse at their head; and they retired, drawing their horses backwards, like the mist on the neighbouring hill, when driven by a sudden gust from the mouth of some narrow glen. The horsemen divided and allowed the men, who had assumed so noble a daring, to pass unmolested through their ranks and to escape, without the firing of a single shot. This was certainly a rare occurrence, and might probably be accounted for, if we were acquainted with all the circumstances of the case.

Michael Smith lived in Quarrel-wood, not far from Dumfries. He kept a small house of entertainment, which was open to all sorts of persons, and among others, to the Covenanters. Michael had a warm side to the persecuted people, and none were more welcome to his little inn than they. He embraced every opportunity of relieving and sheltering them. It was in his power to do this in the character of an inn-keeper, without attaching any suspicion to his conduct, as his house was free to every person. Michael's partiality to the Covenanters, however, became too glaring to pass without notice, and he was complained of as one who harboured the rebels. To ascertain the truth on this point then, a party of dragoons was despatched to Michael's house. He was asked if he entertained any of the disaffected people, and if he received money from them. Smith replied, "that as he kept an inn, however humble in its pretensions, for the accommodation of travellers, he could not tell who they might be that happened to call at his house, nor was it his business to inquire—that he was in the habit of receiving payment from those who were served either with liquor or with food; but if, on any occasion, it turned out that, when the reckoning was called for, some had nothing wherewith to pay, what could he do but let them go?—that it was a hard thing if the poverty of others should be charged as a crime upon him, or that people should say he harboured the Covenanters, simply because he occasionally received nothing from those who had nothing to give." This statement seemed satisfactory to the party; and, in order to end the matter, it was proposed that he should take the test. The test was administered to suspected persons, and was first imposed in 1681. It has been justly characterized as "a medley of Popery, Prelacy, Erastianism, and self-contradiction." It demanded an acknowledgment of the king's supremacy, in all causes ecclesiastical as well as civil, and a renunciation of the covenants and the Presbyterian establishment. "For many years," says Wodrow, "it became a handle for persecuting, even to the death, great numbers, and some of them of very considerable rank; and oppressing multitudes of noblemen, gentlemen, and others, who could not comply with it." Honest Michael Smith objected to the test, chiefly on the ground of his ignorance of its nature, alleging that it was a hard thing to force a man to take a solemn oath, of which he had no competent understanding; and his reasoning, it seems, prevailed, for the matter was no further insisted on. The dragoons having, no doubt, been entertained in a befitting manner by the innkeeper, who had every thing in his possession in the shape of liquors that suited their taste, requested his assistance to enable them to trace their way to the retreat of some Covenanters who were supposed to be lurking in the neighbourhood. It appears that the soldiers frequently forced suspected persons to guide them in their search for the wanderers who were in concealment: th s they did, no doubt, on the supposition that they were well acquainted with their hiding-places; but it generally happened that they were the worst guides they could have chosen, because they were sure, by some means or other, to defeat the end for which they were selected. Michael Smith, on this occasion, accompanied the troopers with no good will to the work on which they were bent. The persons of whom they were in quest were concealed in a wild bosky glen, called the Ballachin wood, through which murmurs a crystal stream of the same name. As they proceeded along, threading their way among the trees and bushes, Smith happened to be considerably in advance, traversing a narrow foot-path that led across the brook. As he walked onward, and the soldiers following his guidance, he plainly perceived, at a short distance before him, and exactly in the track of his route, a man stretched at his full length on the ground and fast asleep. He had no doubt whatever that the man was one of the Covenanters in hiding, and, in all likelihood, one of the very party they were seeking. What was to be done: to advance a few yards further would inevitably lead to a discovery, and to stand still and appear to hesitate would lead to suspicion. In this perplexity Smith had recourse to stratagem; and wheeling round, with his face to the dragoons, cried out, "Do you see that hare?" The soldiers turned to look, and at the moment a hare actually started from the covert near their feet. The circumstance diverted their attention for a while, and afforded the sleeping man time to escape, and to inform his friends of the danger that was approaching. In this way Smith, who became a reluctant guide to the troopers, was the means of saving the persons whom they sought to destroy. Further search, of course, was fruitless; for the party in concealment hastily removed from the spot, to seek elsewhere a place of retreat. Thus the worthy innkeeper had the satisfaction of having, on one and the same day, both extricated himself from a snare, and delivered a company of pious men from death.

On another occasion he was no less successful in saving from their enemies a party of Covenanters in his own house. Three of those men, exhausted with their wanderings, came one evening to his abode, for the purpose of obtaining food and rest. As they were sitting by the fire, after having partaken of a refreshing meal, a detachment of dragoons came galloping to the door. "We are gone," said the men to their landlord; "we shall be captured instantly." "No," replied he, "do as I bid you: here is a sample of malt which I will spread on the table before you, as if you had been examining it, and lean forward on the board, and pretend to be fast asleep." Michael met the dragoons at the door, who asked him if he had any of the Covenanters within? "There are," said he, "three men, who called some time ago: they are in an apartment by themselves, and you can enter and see what you think of them." The dragoons dismounted and followed him to the place where the men were seated, and apparently in a sound sleep, with their heads leaning on the table, and malt spread before them. "You can judge for yourselves," said Smith, "whether these are praying Covenanters, or drunken maltsters; rouse them, and see what they have to say for themselves." The soldiers no sooner saw the state of matters than they turned away, not thinking it worth their while to disturb the repose of the sleeping men after their supposed debauch, and left them to recover themselves at their own convenience. This contrivance was the means of deceiving the troopers, who were withheld from making a particular investigation, which would have doubtless led to a discovery. Thus did Providence throw over these men the shield of protection in the very moment of their imminent danger, and saved them from their enemies, in circumstances in which deliverance appeared almost impossible.

Margaret Smith, a great grand-daughter of Michael Smith, whose memory has supplied these anecdotes of her worthy ancestor, lives at Penpont, and is now an old woman, and full of days.

CHAPTER X.

Thomas Harkness, Andrew Clark, and Samuel McEwan—Daniel McMichael—Babe of Tweedhope-foot—John Hunter.

After the rescue at Enterkin, which took place in the summer of 1684, and of which mention has already been made, the inhabitants of the south and west were subjected to very severe treatment. Orders were issued for assembling all the male population in Nithsdale, above the age of fifteen years, in the different localities appointed, for the purpose of searching the whole county, with a view to apprehend the persons engaged in that enterprise. A meeting was accordingly held in every parish, and a strict search was made in houses, and moors, and woods, but without effect. On the failure of this attempt, it was next agreed on, that a public intimation should be made by the Curates the next Sabbath, in the ten or twelve parishes nearest the scene of the rescue;—that all above fifteen years should meet at New Dalgerno, to answer, upon oath, what questions might be put to them. A great company met at the appointed place, and the following questions were asked:—"Do you know who rescued the prisoners at Enterkin? Do you know which way they fled? Do you know where they are at present?" The multitude which met at Dalgerno was too numerous to be interrogated in one day, and therefore meetings were appointed to be held in the different parishes, where the above questions were to be put to each individual. Those who failed to appear at those meetings were either imprisoned or obliged to keep the soldiers at free quarters for a specified time. This annoying and vexatious work continued for about six weeks; and it is easy to imagine the trouble and distress to which the district in general was exposed. James Harkness of Locherben, and others with him, who were engaged in the affair of the rescue, were apprehended and carried to Edinburgh. Harkness was tried, and condemned to die, but he happily avoided the execution of the sentence, by escaping, along with twenty-five fellow-prisoners, from the Canongate jail. Thomas Harkness, the brother of James, was not so fortunate. He, along with Andrew Clark of Leadhills, and Samuel McEwan of Glencairn, was seized by Claverhouse, when like a fury he was roaming through all the places in Nithsdale, where he hoped to apprehend the rebels who had attacked the king's troops. He came upon the three helpless men, as they were sleeping in the fields, in the parish of Closeburn. They were so fast asleep that the soldiers had to rouse them;

and when they opened their eyes, and saw their enemies standing over them, like ravenous beasts ready to pounce on their prey, they attempted to flee, but in vain, for the soldiers who, on account of the defeat at Enterkin, were exceedingly enraged, wounded them and took them prisoners. Whether any of them were at Enterkin, or not, does not appear; but the soldiers deponed that they were, and therefore they were conveyed to Edinburgh, and were condemned to die on the same day on which they were tried. "They were," says Wodrow, "brought into Edinburgh about one of the clock, and that same day they were sentenced and executed about five of the clock." This evidently shows how eagerly their enemies thirsted for their blood. But though the summons was hasty, they were not unprepared; they lived with death constantly before them, and were in hourly expectation of meeting with the last enemy. Their brethren were daily falling on the moors and hills around them, and therefore they held themselves in constant readiness to meet with a similar fate. The interval between the sentence and execution. was short; but brief as the period was, they drew up a conjunct testimony to that truth in behalf of which they suffered. This testimony, though expressed in a few words, is worthy of notice, and is as follows.

"The joint testimony of Thomas Harkness, An drew Clark, and Samuel McEwan, from the tol booth of Edinburgh, August 5, (1684.)

"Dear friends and relations whatsomever, we think fit to acquaint you, that we bless the Lord that ever we were ordained to give a public testimony, who are so great sinners. Blessed be He hat we were born to bear witness for him, and blessed be the Lord Jesus Christ, that ordained the gospel and the truths of it, which he sealed with his own blood; and many a worthy Christian gone before us hath sealed them. We were questioned for not owning the king's authority. We answered, that we owned all authority that is allowed by the written word of God, sealed by Christ's blood. Now, our dear friends, we entreat you to stand to the truth, and especially all ye that are our own relations, and all that love and wait for the coming of Christ. He will come and not tarry, and reward every one according to their deeds in the body. We bless the Lord that we are not a whit discouraged, but content to lay down our lives with cheerfulness, and boldness, and courage; and if we had a hundred lives, we would willingly quit with them all for the truth of Christ. Good news! Christ is no worse than he promised. Now we take our leave of all our friends and acquaintances, and declare we are heartily content with our lot, and that he hath brought us hither to witness for him and his truth. We leave our testimony against Popery, and all other false doctrine that is not according to the Scriptures of the Old and New Testaments, which is the only word of God. Dear friends, be valiant for God, for he is as good as his promise. Him that overcometh he will make a pillar in his temple. Our time is short, and we have little to spare, having got our sentence at one of the clock this afternoon, and are to die at five this day; and so we will say no more, but farewell all friends and relations, and welcome heaven, and Christ, and the cross, for Christ's sake.

THOMAS HARKNESS,
ANDREW CLARK,
SAMUEL MCEWAN."

In this short statement, emitted by these three plain country men, on the very eve of their death, of which they were not apprized sooner than four brief hours before it happened, we perceive no confusion nor perturbation, but an admirable calmness of spirit, and Christian fortitude, and confidence in God. The peace and evenness of mind which they displayed, proves that the experience of the truth on the heart is a reality, and that the faith of the gospel is capable of sustaining the soul in the most trying and appalling circumstances. Had any of their enemies received the sentence of death in themselves as they did, we can easily conceive the trepidation into which they would have been thrown, and their blank consternation in the immediate prospect of death; for the soul, without hope in God, and a well-grounded confidence in his favour, is, at that solemn moment, like a ship torn from its anchorage, and tossed by the raging winds on the tempestuous bosom of a troubled sea. O how precious is that gospel which supports the soul amid all the cares, and anxieties, and tribulations of life, and at last, in death, soothes the heart into a sweet and holy serenity, which enables the believer to triumph even in the moment of dissolution.

Andrew Clark was a smith in Leadhills, and was a brother to Adam Clark of Glenirn.

Connected with these worthies, in the same cause, and in Christian friendship, was Daniel McMichael, who was shot by Captain Dalziel at Dalveen, in the parish of Durisdeer. The tradition respecting the circumstances of his capture by his enemies, furnishes us with by far the fullest and most correct account of the matter that has hitherto appeared. Daniel McMichael, as has already been noticed in the account given of his brother James, was born at Dalzien on the Water of Scar. We have no notice, however, respecting the time and the manner in which his mind was first savingly impressed with the truth. Whether it was in early youth, or in riper years, that he became the subject of a gracious change, tradition has not informed us. The fact, however, is certain, that he was a true believer, a genuine follower of the Saviour, and that he was honoured to seal his testimony with his blood. From the circumstance of his name being inserted in the fugitive roll, it would appear that his principles as a non-conformist, were well known, and that he was especially marked by his enemies. In the roll referred to, he is designated "Daniel McMichael in Lurgfoot." The place is now called Blairfoot, and belongs to the farm of Burn, in the parish of Morton. In this locality there was a cave by the side of a mountain stream, to which, in those days, the Covenanters often resorted. It was a hallowed retreat to many, not only as a place of refuge from their foes, but as a sanctuary of heavenly fellowship. Daniel McMichael's house at Blairfoot, was something like the house of the good John Brown of Priesthill. It was a little church, a meeting-place to all the religious people in the district who assembled there, for the purpose of Christian fellowship and prayer. The wanderers who had located themselves in the dens and wilds of the neighbouring mountains, frequently stole to Daniel's cottage, to spend the hours of a cold and stormy winter's evening in spiritual intercourse; and many a weary outcast found it a Bethel for God's presence and communion with his saints. In the dreary month of January 1635, Daniel was confined to his bed of a fever, caught it is not said how, but, in all proba bility, brought on by his frequent exposure to cold and wet when he was obliged to withdraw himself from the face of his foes to the bleak and inclement deserts. The worthy men who lay in concealment in the vicinity often visited Daniel in his affliction, and prayed and discoursed like men who were on the wing to a better world. By means of these heavenly communings his spirit was refreshed, and even in his body he felt himself strengthened. One day a company of these pious persons met at Blairfoot for the purpose of engaging in religious exercises, and they adopted the common precaution of stationing a friend as a warder to give notice in case of danger. At this time Captain Dalziel and Lieutenant Straiton with a party of fifty soldiers, were ranging the country in quest of fugitives. Muncie, the informer, had received notice of the meeting that was being held in McMichael's house, and he lost no time in communicating information of the circumstance to the commander of the troops, who led his company without delay to Blairfoot. The watchman, however, observed their approach, and hastened to the house with the unwelcome tidings. The party within instantly prepared for flight, but in their haste to be gone they forgot not their sickly brother. They knew that, if he was left alone, his affliction would procure him no exemption from the ill usage with which the soldiers might be disposed to treat him, and therefore they determined to remove him from his bed, and carry him along with them. Accordingly they wrapped him in the warm bed-clothes, and conveyed him with all speed, and unobserved, to the cave. Here in the dark cold cell they made for him a bed, as soft and comfortable as circumstances would admit of;

and when matters were arranged in the best manner possible, they fled to the hills. Dalziel and his party arrived at Blairfoot, but found nobody. It was obvious that the little conventicle had been warned of their approach, and that in their flight they could not be far distant. The troopers then spread themselves abroad in pursuit of the fugitives, and, whether by accident, or guided by some person who knew the place, they reached the cave in which the sick man was lying. No pity was shown to him in his distressful situation; he was rudely seized, and carried off to Durisdeer, where he remained in custody during the night. Many questions were put to him, which he declined to answer, and many things laid to his charge which he denied. He was told that unless he owned the government in church and state, and took the oath that might be put to him, he must die. "Sir," said he, "that is what in all things I cannot do, but very cheerfully I submit to the Lord's disposal as to my life." Dalziel replied, "Do you not know that your life is in my hand?" "No sir," answered he, "I know that my life is in the Lord's hand, and if he see good he can make you the instrument to take it away." He was told that he might prepare for death, for he should die on the morrow. To this he said, "If my life must go for his cause, I am willing; my God will prepare me." The night before his death, "he enjoyed," says Wodrow, "a sweet time of communion and fellowship with God, and great outlets of joy and consolation, so that some of the soldiers desired to die his death, and not a few convictions were left in their bosoms." By this means the Lord strengthened his servant whom he called forth to witness for his truth, and prepared him with spiritual fortitude, and hope, and joy, for the endurance of the trial which was before him. Next day he was conducted to Dalveen, the fields of which were to be converted into the scene of a bloody tragedy, and from which his ransomed soul, "from insult springing," was to ascend to the throne of God to obtain the martyr's crown. When he arrived at the spot, sickly and feeble, he was permitted to engage for a brief space in those devotional exercises which were befitting a person in his situation, a favour not granted to every one. When he had ended his devotions, he addressed himself in a very grave and solemn manner to Dalziel, who had lent himself to work wickedness, and to make havoc of the Church. What impression his discourse made on the captain's mind is not said, but he shrunk not from the perpetration of the deed which he meditated. When the napkin was tied round his face, this faithful witness for Christ, who loved not his life unto the death, lifted up his voice, and said aloud, "Lord, thou broughtest Daniel through many trials, and hast brought me, thy servant, hither to witness for thee and thy cause; into thy hands I commit my spirit, and hope to praise thee through all eternity." The signal was then given, and four soldiers poured the contents of their muskets into his body, and the warm blood flowed from the wounds in purple streams on the grassy sod. The green heights of Dalveen resounded with the startling report, and the echo leaped from hill to hill, as if to announce to those who dwelt afar in the wilderness that another honoured witness for the truth had fallen. His pains were of short continuance, and his happy spirit, emancipated from its frail tenement, exulted in its victory over death, and winged its way to the regions of eternal repose. His memory is still warmly cherished by the people of the neighbourhood, whose boast it is that his ashes rest in their church-yard, and that the spot on which he fell is pointed out by a suitable monument.

Among the spectators who were present witnessing this atrocious murder, was a boy, named John McCall, from Dalzien, the place of Daniel's nativity. There happened to be lying on the grass near the bleeding body of the martyr, a small wooden basin, called by the peasantry, a *luggie.* The captain commanded the boy, who was standing by, to take the vessel, and to run to the well to fetch him water to wash from his hands and clothes the blood that had spurted from the wounds of the slaughtered man, whom, in his contemptuous style, he denominated a *dog.* The boy, with the mingled feelings of indignation and terror, seized the luggie and ran towards the well, but, instead of fetching water, he dashed it into the limpid fountain, and flew to the hills. The insulted commander ordered the troopers to pursue and fire on the fugitive. They did so, but he was young and agile, and, like the fleet roe, he bounded away, and left the dragoons far behind in the hopeless pursuit. This boy was the great-grandfather of the worthy tenant who at present occupies the Holm of Drumlanrig.

Daniel McMichael was a man of eminent godliness and simplicity of character. He lived but for one thing, namely, to honour Him who had called him out of darkness into his marvellous light. Having embraced the truth in the love of it, he adhered to it with constancy, and at the hazard of all he held dearest on earth, he followed Christ, his great leader, wherever he conducted him. And he whom he followed through life, did not forsake him in death; for when he was called to suffer, he wanted not that support, and those consolations, which are necessary to fortify the heart in the hour of trial. His faith in the Redeemer, and the comforts of the Holy Spirit, enabled him to triumph over death, and to afford to those who witnessed his tragical end, a proof of the reality of that religion, in the profession of which he lived and died.

The account of the death of John Hunter of Tweedsmuir, may follow as an appropriate sequel to the story of Daniel McMichael. There lived, in this remote and muirland district, a man of the name of Welsh, commonly called "the Babe of Tweedhope-foot." How he acquired this nickname it is not easy to say, but he was a man of very great bodily strength; and stories are told of his wonderful feats, that seem to partake more of legend than of sober truth. He was, however, identified with the Covenanters: his house was a home to the ministers, and he had suffered many privations on account of the sympathy which he showed them. Having heard that Colonel James Douglas was in the neighbourhood, and justly suspecting that he would not leave the district without paying him a visit, he determined to withdraw to the wilds for concealment. He was accompanied by John Hunter, a native of the same place, a good man and a zealous Covenanter. The place to which they resorted was the solitudes of Corehead, near the source of the Water of Annan. Douglas, however, having got notice of their flight, pursued them with his troop, and soon gained ground on the fugitives. When they saw that there was a likelihood of their being overtaken, they directed their course to a place called the "Straught Steep," which, being difficult of access to the dragoons, they expected would afford them a safe retreat. By this time the horsemen were very near, and began to fire upon them. Hunter, who it seems was fully within the reach of the shot, was struck by a ball which proved fatal. He fell among the stones over which he was scrambling, and his life's blood oozed forth upon the rocks, where he expired. His body was removed, and interred in the church-yard of Tweedsmuir. His death took place in 1685, the "black year." This good man, who was suddenly taken away by a violent death, had no time afforded him to pray, or to compose his mind, before his immediate entrance into eternity; but then he was habitually prepared, and living, it may be, in the constant expectation of a hasty summons into the other world, he was always ready for his departure. "Be ye also ready, for in such an hour as ye think not, the Son of man cometh."

After the death of his companion, Welsh continued his flight across the wilderness, intending, if possible, to reach a place called Carterhope. He arrived at the house without having been seen by the troopers, and placed himself by the fire, to wait the result. The soldiers, though they did not see him enter, had nevertheless followed in the track in which he had fled, and at length came to the place. They entered in their usually uproarious manner, while Welsh was sitting apparently unconcerned before the fire. The soldiers not expecting perhaps to find the object of their pursuit in the hut, and having no personal knowledge of him, did not seem to notice him. The mistress of the house, however, fearing lest a discovery should by some means be made, resorted to a kind of stratagem to prevent suspicion. She approached Welsh, who appeared to be carelessly dozing over the fire, and giving him a heavy slap between the shoulders, commanded him to rise and to proceed to his work, chiding him for his slothfulness in sitting all day cowering by the hearth, while his proper business was neglected. He took the hint, and withdrew from the apartment. The soldiers naturally conceived that he was a person belonging to the house, and consequently made no inquiries. He often remarked, that the kindest *cuff* he ever received was from the gudewife of Carterhope, whose presence of mind, at that critical moment, was in all likelihood the means of saving his life.

CHAPTER XI.

Thomas Hutchison—Marion Cameron—Margaret Wilson.

The farm of Daljig, in the neighbourhood of the village of New Cumnock in Ayrshire, was in the times of persecution occupied by Thomas Hutchison. This locality, as was formerly noticed, was the scene of much suffering on the part of the people of God, and consequently of much oppressive dealing on the part of their enemies. Claverhouse, in his raids through Nithsdale, often visited this quarter, and spread distress among the simple-minded and virtuous inhabitants. From the two garrisons that were placed in Carsfairn, bands of troopers were constantly passing down the romantic defile of the Afton, and across the country by the two Cumnocks, to the different stations in the route to the lower parts of Clydesdale. These military parties, we may easily suppose, never passed the hamlets and cottages of the peasantry without mischief, and many an unwary Covenanter was shot by them in the open fields, or seized in the privacy of their domestic dwellings. The country people that lay on the different tracts between the numerous garrisons with which the south and the west was so thickly studded, could never deem themselves secure for a single day from the intrusion of the strolling companies that were perpetually in motion, and to whose rudeness and insolence there were no bounds. The licentious manner in which the soldiers behaved is scarcely credible. Claverhouse, in making his descent on Dumfriesshire from the west, along the line of the Nith sometimes in the mere wantonness of his authority drove before him indiscriminately the inhabitants on both sides of the river, like a flock of sheep, and then apprehended or dismissed them at his pleasure.

It was when one of these lawless bands was passing through the higher parts of Kyle, that Thomas Hutchison made a narrow escape for his life. He was a very young man, and at an early period of his days became a subject of Divine grace. We are not to suppose that those who adhered to the principles of the honest Covenanters were merely aged men, or even persons in the middle stage of life: there were also many youthful persons, of both sexes, who valiantly contended for the cause of righteousness and of liberty. Nor were these young witnesses actuated simply by a bigoted preference to the opinions of their fathers, irrespective of the justness of their opinions; they knew and understood the ground on which they stood, and were prepared, at any hazard, to maintain the cause they had espoused. It is a delightful and animating spectacle to witness those who are in the morning and bloom of their days, seeking the Lord, and devoting themselves to his service. Such a sight is ever stimulating to those who are advanced in the Christian life, and whose years and experience have imparted to them more solidity and strength. The reality of a religious profession was in those days tested to the utmost; for the sufferings and trials to which godly persons were uniformly subjected, operated as a sufficient preventive in hindering those who had only a name to live, from connecting themselves with a party that was environed with so much tribulation.

The youth and simplicity of Thomas Hutchison were no defence against the persecuting spirit of the times in which he lived, and therefore the enemies of that cause which he had espoused determined to show him no favour. The dragoons, in their approach to Daljig, were seen by young Hutchison, who at that time happened to be on the moor and at a considerable distance from the dwelling-house. He knew the purport of their visit, and he was fully aware of the fate that awaited him if he should fall into their hands, and therefore he determined to secure his safety by flight. Accordingly, he directed his steps to a thicket, in the neighbourhood of which he expected to find a place of concealment from the face of his pursuers. He therefore ran at his utmost speed towards the woody retreat; but there is little likelihood that he would have attained his object, had not Providence placed unexpected help within his reach. As he was hastening with youthful agility and velocity along the bent, he observed before him a young and spirited horse grazing on the heath to which, as was customary, he had been driven after the season of labour was past. Hutchison sprang forward, and, grasping the horse firmly by the mane, vaulted him at one bound. He had no bridle by which to guide the motions of the animal, but, by slapping with his hand on the head and neck, he succeeded in directing him to the right and left as necessity required. The fleet and willing steed carried him before his pursuers, till he reached the edge of the thicket in which he intended to secrete himself. By this time the troopers were fast approaching. They had commenced the chase the moment they saw him begin to run, for they naturally concluded that none but Covenanters would flee from them; and hence the slightest symptom of timidity, or any attempt at flight, was on every occasion a signal of pursuit. When Hutchison arrived at the covert, he instantly dismounted and plunged into the heart of the dense bushes; but before he had time to conceal himself from their view, the horsemen came up. They did not venture into the thicket lest they should entangle themselves in the underwood, or otherwise bewilder themselves; but drawing their pistols from their holsters, they shot after him with vehemence. The leaden bullets went whizzing and booming past his head among the rustling leaves and thick branches of the wood. Not one of the fatal messengers, however, that were sent after him, touched his person, and he escaped unscathed into the heart of the retreat. Providence threw over him a broad shield of safety in the hour of peril, and heard his cry in the day of his distress.

The soldiers, when they saw that the prey had escaped them, turned away baffled and chagrined, and prepared to wreak their vengeance with greater fury on the next suspected person they should meet. Hutchison remained in his hiding-place till the storm for the present had blown over, and he returned to his father's house to receive the congratulations of his friends, and to thank the God in whom he trusted for the special deliverance vouchsafed. Tradition has not retained any other incident respecting this youthful Covenanter, though doubtless many interesting occurrences must have befallen him during the trying times in which his lot was cast. He outlived the persecution for many a long year, and maintained till the end of his days a character consistent with his profession. His religious example was followed by his descendants, who grew up around him in the fear of God, and his posterity have still a name and a place in the church of Christ.

But though Thomas Hutchison escaped on this occasion the murderous hands of his foes, yet others of the wanderers in the same neighbourhood shared a very different fate. There is a melancholy story related of Marion Cameron, sister to the celebrated Richard Cameron, who fell at Airs moss. Marion Cameron, it appears, was a pious young woman, and sincerely attached to the cause of the persecuted. Her brother lost his life in 1680, from which period onward to the Revolution the furnace of persecution glowed with a much fiercer heat than formerly. Murders were now common in the fields, and many were shot by the soldiers without trial, and even without warning. It appears that Marion Cameron, with two other individuals, had been surprised by a party of dragoons, and had fled for their lives in the direction of Daljig. They hid themselves in a moss in the vicinity, and being overpowered with fatigue, they cowered down to rest. In this situation, helpless and exposed, they engaged in prayer, and resigned themselves entirely to the disposal of Him in whose cause they were suffering, and for whose sake they were willing to lay down their lives. Having been refreshed with the consolations of that gracious Spirit by whose influences they were enabled to approach the mercy-seat with the voice of supplication, they rose from their knees, and raised to Heaven the serene and melodious sound of praise, in chanting one of the Psalms of the sweet singer of Israel, which seemed to be adapted to persons in their situation. And many are the Psalms that are suited to God's church in affliction; for he who wrote them was himself one who suffered persecution, and who had often to betake himself to the dens and caves of the earth for safety. The troopers who, on this occasion, followed them, could not fail to be guided by the plaintive and hallowed sound, which issued from the little company of worshippers in the morass, to the very spot where they had hid themselves. On their approach they offered them their lives, on condition, it is said, that they would burn their Bibles. Such a proposal, revolting to their holiest feelings, they rejected with abhorrence, and were willing, far more willing, to part with their lives, than to desecrate the word of God—that word of grace, by the consolations of which they were supported in their sufferings, and by the faith of which they hoped to be saved. The troopers well knew that this proposal would be rejected, but then it served as an additional pretext, on their part, to proceed to extremi ties. Accordingly they avowed their intention to shoot them on the spot, as persons who refused to obey the king's authority, in this as well as in other respects. There was no alternative; the defenceless company in the moss could not yield, and they could not escape, and therefore instant death was inevitable. The dragoons then without the slightest feeling of compassion, immediately prepared the instruments of death; they fired, and all the three fell prostrate on the heath, and the warm purple stream of life mingled with the dark moss water in the moor, and their redeemed spirits were conveyed by angels from their mangled bodies to the mansion of eternal blessedness. Their enemies appeared to conquer, but they who fell were really the victors, for "they overcame by the blood of the Lamb, and by the word of their testimony, for they loved not their lives unto the death."

They suffered martyrdom in a place where there were no earthly spectators present to sympathize with them, and they were buried in their clothes in the moss where they fell; and, as "devout men carried Stephen to his burial, and made great lamentation over him," so the friends of these Christian confessors came, when their enemies had retired from the spot, and dug their graves in the morass, in which they laid their murdered bodies, to rest till the morning of the general resurrection. "Blessed are the dead who die in the Lord from henceforth; yea, saith the Spirit, that they may rest from their labours, and their works do follow them."

The sweet and gentle Marion Cameron, like a delicate and lovely flower, was, in the bloom of her days, despoiled of her life by the rough and pitiless hand of violence. She has a name among the "many daughters who have done virtuously," and she, with her companions, has obtained the martyr's crown, and now are they with the multitude who have suffered for "the word of God and for the testimony of Jesus Christ.' How enviable is the situation of the persecuted, even in their greatest afflictions, compared with that of their oppressors, even in their greatest prosperity. The triumph of the wicked is short, while their ruin is endless and irremediable: on the other hand, in the case of the righteous, their "light affliction, which is but for a moment, worketh out for them a far more exceeding, and an eternal weight of glory."

About seventy years ago, while some cattle were trampling in the moss exactly over the graves of those worthies, their feet turned up part of the clothes of Marion Cameron, which were then in a tolerably good state of preservation, owing to the antiseptic quality of the moss in which they were imbedded; and a large common yellow pin, which she was accustomed to wear in her raiment, was found and cherished as a precious relic of one whose memory was held so dear. The pin came into the possession of Mrs. Gemmel, of Catrine, a niece of Thomas Hutchison of Daljig, by whom it was retained all her days, as a precious memorial of the original proprietor. It is now in the possession of a daughter of Mrs. Gemmel's, who at present resides at Stranraer, by whom it is preserved with equal care.

The murder of such saintly persons as Marion Cameron, depicts, in colours sufficiently glaring, the dark and revolting barbarity of the times. The sun in the firmament scarcely ever beheld deeds of greater atrocity, than those committed by the rude and hardened troopers, on the unoffending peasantry of Scotland. But the case of Marion Cameron was not a solitary one; there are other instances of young and timid females who exhibited the greatest firmness and moral heroism, in enduring sufferings for Christ's sake. The case of Margaret Wilson, who at the age of eighteen years was drowned in the sea near Wigton, in Galloway, for her non-conformity, is an illustrious instance, and it will require no apology to present the reader with a brief account of her martyrdom, as given by Wodrow. She, along with one Margaret McLaughlan, a mother in Israel, of about sixty-three years of age, the widow of John Mulligen, a carpenter in the parish of Kirkinner, in Galloway, was sentenced to be drowned within the tide-mark in the Water of Blednock, near Wigton. During the time they lay in prison, "Margaret Wilson's friends," says Wodrow, "used all means to prevail with her to take the abjuration oath, and to engage to hear the Curate, but she stood fast in her integrity, and would not be shaken. They received their sentence with a great deal of composure and cheerful countenances, reckoning it their honour to suffer for Christ and his truth. During her imprisonment, Margaret Wilson wrote a large letter to her relations, full of a deep and affecting sense of God's love to her soul, and an entire resignation to the Lord's disposal. She likewise added a vindication of her refusing to save her life, by taking the abjuration, and engaging to conformity; against both she gives argument, with a solidity and judgment far above her years and education.

"This barbarous sentence," continues the historian, "was executed May 11th, and the two women were brought from Wigton, with a numerous crowd of spectators to witness so extraordinary an execution. Major Windram, with some soldiers, guarded them to the place of execution. The old woman's stake was a good way in beyond the other; and she was first despatched, in order to terrify the other to a compliance with such oaths and conditions as they required—but in vain, for she adhered to her principles with unshaken steadfastness. When the water was overflowing her fellow martyr, some about Margaret Wilson asked her what she thought of the other, now struggling with the pangs of death. She answered, 'What do I see but Christ in one of his members wrestling there? Think you that we are the sufferers? no, it is Christ in us, for he sends none a warfare upon their own charges.' When Margaret Wilson was at the stake, she sang the 25th Psalm, from verse 7 downwards a good way, and read the 8th chapter of the Romans, with a great deal of cheerfulness, and then prayed. While at prayer the water covered her, but before she was quite dead they pulled her up and held her out of the water, till she was recovered and able to speak, and then, by Major Windram's orders, she was asked if she would pray for the king: she answered, she 'wished the salvation of all men, and the damnation of none.' One deeply affected with the death of the other, and her case, said, 'Dear Margaret, say, God save the king—say, God save the king.' She answered, in the greatest steadiness and composure, "God save him if he will, for it is his salvation I desire." Whereupon some of her relations near by, desirous to have her life spared if possible, called out to Major Windram, 'Sir, she hath said it, she hath said it.' Whereupon the Major came near, and offered her the abjuration, charging her instantly to swear it, otherwise to return to the water. Most deliberately she refused, and said, 'Let me go, I am one of Christ's children ; let me go.' Upon which she was thrust down again into the water, where she finished her course with joy. She died a virgin martyr, about eighteen years of age ; and both of them suffered precisely upon refusing conformity and the abjuration oath, and were evidently innocent of any thing worthy of death ; and since properly they suffered upon refusing the abjuration, for the refusing of which multitudes were cut off in the fields with less ceremony, and at the time when these murders were so common, I have brought them in here."

Such instances of barbarity show the reckless and unprincipled character of those who were deputed by the equally unprincipled and worthless rulers of that period, to do that work of wickedness to which Satan prompted them. But while such deeds of violence depict the character of those who perpetrated them, and hold them up in a very despicable light to posterity, they who suffered displayed a very different character. Their meekness, their constancy, their blameless deportment, the strength of their faith and hope in God, their confidence in the goodness of their cause, their joy in the Redeemer, and their firmness of purpose in the hour of death, were all displayed in an eminent degree, illustrative of the grace of God, which wrought so powerfully in them, to the entire discomfiture of their foes, who, though they killed the body, could not vanquish their principles.

CHAPTER XII.

Lesmahagow—Thomas Brown, of Auchlochan—Smith of Threepod—John Gill—Stobo,

Lesmahagow is a name familiar to all who are in any measure versant in the times and scenes of prelatic violence. Few sections of the country, perhaps, furnished a richer harvest of godly persons, among whom to thrust the bloody sickle of persecution; and nobly did these honoured persons maintain their fidelity, and the credit of that cause to which they were attached. The moorlands of Lesmahagow, if they could speak, could tell many a tale of suffering now unknown, and could also recount many a blessed hour of sacred intercourse with God, enjoyed by his people in the day of privation and of peril. The inhabitants of this district seem, in the days of Zion's affliction, to have been favoured with large communications of Divine influence, and with much spiritual fortitude, in the hour of temptation. The Steels of Lesmahagow were men of renown, and faithful witnesses for Jesus Christ. The death of David Steel, who was shot at Shellyhill in 1686, in the thirty-third year of his age, is, in all its circumstances, equally affecting with the death of John Brown of Priesthill. He was, after promise of quarter, murdered before his own door; and Mary Wier, his youthful and truly Christian wife, who, it is said, cherished an uncommon attachment to her husband, having bound up his shattered head with a napkin and closed down his eyelids with her own hand, looking on the manly and honest countenance that was now pale in death, said, with a sweet and heavenly composure, "the archers have shot at thee, my husband, but they could not reach thy soul; it has escaped like a dove far away, and is at rest." What is it but the reality of religion that can so fully sustain the hearts of God's people in the day of their tribulation, and under the pressure of afflictions so overwhelming?

The tale of the martyrs of Lesmahagow has been told by a descendant of one of themselves—the Rev. Charles Thomson of North Shields. In the excellent and heart-stirring narrative which he has given of these worthies, we see, on their part, the display of a genuine godliness, of a patient endurance of trial, and of an unflinching constancy of purpose, even to the death, of a most instructive nature, and which, placed in contrast with the conduct of their heartless oppressors, points them out as the excellent ones of the earth, and as men of whom the world was not worthy.

Of the confessors of Lesmahagow, however, there are yet some gleanings, which have not hitherto been made public, one of which shall be given here:—Thomas Brown of Auchlochan, in the parish of Lesmahagow, was a good man and a steady Covenanter. He was present at Drumclog, where the fierce Claverhouse sustained a signal defeat by a handful of worshippers, who had been holding a conventicle near the place, on Sabbath, the 1st of June, 1679. He fought also at Bothwell bridge, where the power of the Covenanters was lamentably broken, and their army scattered. If, prior to the rising at Bothwell, the furnace of persecution glowed with an intolerable heat, it was now kindled seven times; and the cloud that owered over the afflicted church, grew darker and more portentous, and threatened to discharge its ominous contents, in one full and vengeful tempest, on the defenceless heads of those who had hitherto outbraved the fury of the storm, in the support of their civil and religious privileges. At this period Claverhouse was ravaging the west, and, like a beast of prey, was tearing and devouring on all sides; for that reckless and infatuated cavalier would not have scrupled to ride, even to the bridle reins, in the blood of the populace, to serve the vindictive purposes of his military employers; and much and precious was the blood which, with unsparing hand, he shed in the fields and moorlands, and loud was the cry which his oppression made to ascend from many a cottage in the land. Two of the troopers under the command of this bloodthirsty adventurer, came suddenly upon Thomas Brown, on the banks of the Nethan, a few yards above the house of Auchlochan. Brown stood on his defence, and with his drawn sword, warded off for some time the blows of his antagonists. At length, however, he was overpowered, and falling under the heavy strokes of the two powerful troopers, he was left for dead on the field. At this juncture, the appearance of another Covenanter on the opposite side of the stream attracted their notice, and leaving their victim bleeding on the ground, they crossed the river in pursuit. This man, whose name is not mentioned, was speedily overtaken, and killed on the spot. Thomas Brown, however, though severely wounded, was not dead. He was stupefied by the loss of blood, and stunned by the blows he had received; but, by the kind attention of his friends, he gradually recovered. He was at this time in the flower of his age, and he lived till he became an old man. The presen' proprietor of Auchlochan is his lineal descendant. It is no small honour to be sprung from those who, in their day, were distinguished as Christ's witnesses, and counted worthy to suffer for his sake. The worth of ancestry, however, will not save us: we must ourselves become followers of them who, through faith and patience, are now inheriting the promises.

The following anecdote refers to a striking incident which took place near the village of Galston, in Ayrshire. Ayrshire was at an early period visited with the gospel. The Culdees and the Lollards of Kyle, in different ages overspread this district, and disseminated the principles of religious truth among its population; and the doctrines of the gospel, thus promulgated in this locality, were never entirely suppressed, either by the superstition of the dark ages, or by the strong arm of persecution. Several years prior to the Reformation, we find that a goodly number of influential individuals in that county had embraced tenets entirely opposed to the Popish creed, and in unison with the pure faith of the gospel. "We find that, in 1494, Robert Blackatter, the first Archbishop of Glasgow, caused to be summoned before the King and his great Council held there, about thirty individuals in all, and mostly persons of distinction, accused of Reformation principles. Among these were George Campbell of Cesnock, Adam Reid of Barskimming, John Campbell of New Mills, Andrew Sharp of Polkemmet, Lady Pokellie, and Lady Stair. They were opprobriously called Lollards of Kyle, from Lollard, an eminent preacher among the Waldenses, and were charged, under thirty-four articles, with maintaining that images ought not to be worshipped—that the relics of saints ought not to be adored—and such like obnoxious tenets; but to these accusations they answered with such boldness, constancy, and effect, that the archbishop and his associates were at length constrained to drop the proceedings; and it was judged most prudent to dismiss them, with the simple admonition to content themselves with the faith of the church, and to beware of new doctrines."

It was from the lower and more level parts of Ayrshire, that many of the refugees that were found seeking a retreat in the higher and more hilly districts, had come. They sought among the inhabitants of Nithsdale and Lanarkshire, that repose which could not be obtained in a more exposed and accessible locality.

Threepod is a farm about two miles from the village of Galston. It was, in the time of persecution, occupied by a worthy man of the name of Smith. He was a person, it would appear, of quiet and retired habits, and had cherished secretly, for some time, the principles of the Covenanters. His natural timidity prevented him for a while from making an open and manly avowal of his sentiments. At length he became decided, and firmly took his stand on the side of the oppressed; and resolved on following what appeared to him to be the plain dictates of duty, and to abide the consequences. In Smith's family there was an infant child, which it was the desire of the parents to devote, as soon as an opportunity offered, to the Lord in baptism. There was, it would seem, about the distance of fourteen miles from Threepod, a conventicle meeting, which was held in the night season. To this meeting Smith carried his child to be baptized by the officiating minister. Having obtained his errand, he retraced his steps through the dreary moors in the dark night; and having arrived at his own house before the dawn, he, in order to prevent suspicion, betook himself to the barn, and was thrashing his corn at the early hour at which labourers generally commence that occupation. In spite of all his caution, however, he had been discovered, and information communicated to his enemies. When he saw that the circumstance was known, and that evil was determined against him, he withdrew from his house, and sought a hiding-place in the fields. Here also his retreat was found out, and two soldiers were sent to apprehend him. On their approach, however, he stood to defend himself; and having in his hand a good broad sword, he succeeded in warding off the deadly blows of his ruthless assailants. He was a young and powerful man, and showed himself capable of wielding, with great dexterity, the sword in self-defence; and the soldiers, finding that he was not to be so easily handled as they expected, had recourse to stratagem. The plan, however, which they adopted, in order to defeat him, was any thing but honourable. When he was engaged in defending himself, and when all his attention was directed to the opponent with whom he was obliged to cope face to face, the other soldier stole behind him, and, approaching with cautious step, threw a cloak over his head, which both blindfolded him and entangled his sword-arm, so that on the instant he became an easy prey to his cruel and wily foes. When the soldiers found that he was now entirely in their power, they hewed him down without mercy, and left him lifeless on the field. They gained their object, but in a way that no noble-minded soldier would choose: they were however, base men, and therefore fitted for the perpetration of the base actions in which their base rulers so fully employed them. This martyr was buried on the spot where his blood was shed—a stone, with an inscription, was laid upon his grave, which is now overgrown with moss; but a thicket of whins, the prickly guardians of his lonely sepulchre, marks the place where his ashes rest. Thus fell an honest patriot and a true Christian, whose constancy of principle and of purpose exposed him to a cruel death.

John Gill lived in Fife, and was, on account of his attachment to reformation principles, subjected to the same treatment as his fellow Covenanters, who received no favour from the hand of those who, in that dark and troubled time, made such fearful havoc of the church of God. The district of Fife, generally, was more immediately under the eye of the Archbishop of St. Andrews, the bloody and perfidious James Sharp, who basely betrayed the cause he was employed to advocate, and ultimately became Primate of the Episcopal Church of Scotland. He obtained the object of his ambition to be sure, but at the expense of a good conscience. He scrupled not to shed profusely the blood of the best and the holiest men the land could boast of; and as he loved to spill blood, so his own blood was spilt at last, and he was slain on Magus-moor as he was lolling in his chariot, in the plenitude of his lordly arrogance and pride. His dream, when a student, as related by Kirkton, which, if real, is curious; and the coincidence of events in his after life, of which it seemed to be indicative, is rather striking. The dream was the following—"That while a student at the college, lying in bed with his comrade, he fell into a loud laughter in his sleep, and being awakened by his bedfellow, who asked him what he laughed so much for, returned answer, that he had dreamed that the Earl of Crawford had made him parson of Crail. Again, in another night, he laughed in his sleep; and being awaked, in like manner, he said he had dreamed he was in paradise, as the king had made him Archbishop of St. Andrews. Lastly, he dreamt a third time, and was in great agony, crying bitterly, when, being awaked as formerly, he said he was dreaming a very sad dream, that he was driving in a coach to hell, and that very fast." Such is the dream, as given by Kirkton. It is certain that he became minister of Crail, and then Primate of St. Andrews; and lastly, that he met his death, while journeying in his coach, on Magus-moor.

John Gill possessed a small paternal estate in Fife, but was obliged to abandon it, and all his property, to preserve his life and a good conscience. He was a good man, and actuated by high principles and unbending religious integrity. The harassings which he underwent from the enemy, instead of weakening his attachment to the cause of Christ, served rather to confirm him in his adherence to the truth—like the oak on the mountain's brow, which, the more it is exposed to the storms above, strikes its roots more deeply and firmly into the soil beneath, so that every succeeding blast leaves it more securely rooted than before. Being obliged to flee from his native place, he went southward, and sought refuge somewhere about the Pentland hills. As tradition has recorded but little respecting this worthy man, it is not known whether he suffered death by the hand of his enemies; but if he outlived the persecution, it is certain that he never regained the possession of his patrimony. But what although he did not? it is better to lose all, than to lose the soul. "Every one that hath forsaken *houses*, or brethren, or sisters, or father, or mother, or wife, or children, or *lands*, for my name's sake, shall receive an hundred fold, and shall inherit everlasting life."

John Gill had a son of the same name, who was illustrious for his piety, which, like a blaze of light, shone so clearly around, that it attracted the notice, and admiration of all within the circle of his acquaintance. His death-bed experience was of the most edifying description, and it is affirmed that he anticipated the very hour of his dissolution, and expired at the time he mentioned, rejoicing in hope of the glory of God. He lived after the persecution, and occupied the farm of Loan-stane, in the neighbourhood of his father's place of refuge; and, if report tells right, he was the first that ploughed the field of Rullion-green, many years after the battle, and that he raked together into heaps the bones of the worthies who fell there, and then buried them deep below the surface. This John Gill the son had two daughters, Catherine and Christian, both of whom walked in the footsteps of their godly parent. Catherine was good and kind, and being a woman of much affliction, profited under the chastising rod. Christian was a mother in Israel, and was more of an influential and commanding manner. As she grew in years, she advanced in grace. She was married to John Ketchan, overseer to Sir James Montgomery of Stobo, a gentleman of no small note in his time, and who by his talents and industry attained both wealth and reputation. John Ketchan was a man of sincere godliness, and of singular integrity in all his dealings, and possessed the unbounded confidence of his master. This worthy man died in 1809, and was interred in the church-yard of Stobo, not far from the more magnificent resting place of his honoured master, whom for many a long year he had served with unswerving fidelity.

The parish of Stobo is a delightful locality on the Tweed, a few miles above the pleasant town of Peebles. The church of Stobo is an edifice of upwards of five hundred years old. The rectory of Stobo was, more than five centuries ago, converted into a prebend of Glasgow; and of all the prebends in Tweeddale, Stobo was reckoned the most valuable. "Michael de Dunde, the parson of Stubbehou or Stobo, swore fealty to Edward the First, at Berwick, on the 2d of August 1296, when the oaths of smaller men were sought for. The rights of the manor of Stobo have been as fiercely contested as the sovereignty of Scotland." The whole parish presents a beautiful aspect; the hills are of a moderate height, and well wooded; the valleys are in the highest state of cultivation, and the centre of the locality is graced with the princely residence of the proprietor. The church is situated near the margin of a silvery stream, which issues from the hills on the back ground, and pours its limpid waters into the Tweed. The burying-ground contains some few antiquities, and preserves the dust of remote and forgotten generations, having been a place of sepulture for many ages. A more sweetly sequestered spot can scarcely be desired; and the man who would wish to shut himself up in a studious seclusion, could not find a retreat more congenial to his taste.

From the summit of Dramore hill, in this neighbourhood, from whose bowels there has been disinterred for sundry ages the fine blue slate stone, a very magnificent view is obtained, especially toward the west. The spacious plain of Drummelzier-haugh, like the level bottom of a deep basin, encircled by green mountains, through which the classic Tweed holds its majestic course, furnishes an enchanting spectacle. On the upper part of this plain, and near the church of Drummelzier, is the grave of the far-famed prophet, *Merlin*, who flourished in the sixth century. The verdant fields of Altarstone and Dreva occupy the sunny slope, whose base is swept by the flowing stream, and front the frowning heights of ancient Dalwick. This locality, no doubt, could once have furnished incidents of persecuting outrage, which are now forgotten. But there can be little dispute that the *nineteen towns* of Stobo contained some whose religious principles subjected them to the treatment common to all, who, during that period, maintained the practice of conscientious non-conformists. Sir William Murray of Stenhope was empowered, in the persecuting times, to exercise a strict supervision over the upper district of Tweeddale; and this power, we may rest assured, was not conferred without a reason.. Symptoms of dissatisfaction had shown themselves, which rendered necessary this military oversight—a proof that the spirit of religious liberty and independence was stirring among this secluded population. In the roll of the ministers who were ejected for their non-conformity to Prelacy, we find the names of Patrick Fleming of Stobo, Robert Brown of Lyne, and David Thompson of Dalwick. These parishes lying together in a cluster, and favoured with a sound gospel ministry at the time of the Restoration, must have contained many whose principles were akin to those of their ministers; and hence a field was prepared on which the persecutor might exercise his intolerance and oppression. In the fugitive roll, we find the name of one man belonging to this parish, "William Forbes, servant to Thomas Weir in Slate-hole." This worthy man, perhaps, was not solitary, though the names of others are not mentioned.

CHAPTER XIII.

Martyrdom at Crossgellioch—Hugh Hutchison—Campbell of Dalhanna—Hair and Corson—Brown and Morice.

"Some time this summer," (1685) says Wodrow, "four men were coming from Galloway, where they had been hearing Mr. Renwick in the fields, to the Shire of Ayr—Joseph Wilson, John and Alexander Jamisons, and John Humphrey. A party of soldiers overtook them at Knockdon-hill, and upon their confessing that they had been hearing a sermon, they immediately shot three of them. What were the reasons of sparing Alexander Jamison, I know not." Such is the account given by the historian of the death of these martyrs—the tradition, however, is much more valuable than the meagre outline of the historic narrative.

Crossgellioch, and not Knockdon-hill, was the place where these martyrs fell, and where they lie interred. Knockdon, however, is in the immediate neighbourhood. Crossgellioch is an oblong hill on the farm of Daljig, situated on the western boundary of the upland parish of New Cumnock.

The ascent on three sides is very steep, but on the north, the declivity is gentle. The top of the hill is generally flat, and interspersed with deep and rugged moss hags, which were frequently occupied as hiding-places by the worthies of the suffering period. It was in the broken morass, on the summit of this mountain, that the individuals above mentioned sought, about the time that they were slaughtered by their enemies, a hiding-place. They had formerly sought a retreat in a place called Tod Fauld, below Benbeoch-craig, where they lay for some time; but being informed by one Paterson, who was himself a refugee, that a reward was offered for their apprehension, they retired to the more secluded locality of Crossgellioch. It was in this place that they were ultimately found, after having one day returned from a conventicle in Carsfairn. Claverhouse, it appears, had been in the pursuit of the wanderers in that neighbourhood; and they, in order to elude his search, took up their accustomed abode among the dark and shaggy heath on the mountain. In this seclusion they remained for several weeks in comparative safety, because, from their lurking-place, they had a view all around, and therefore they could easily perceive the approach of the enemy. This shelter became to them a place of encampment, from which they sallied out at convenient times to visit their brethren in the country around. In this way they could occasionally hold intercourse with their fellow-sufferers, and also furnish themselves with provisions, on which to subsist in their solitude. Their hiding place, it would seem, was known to none in the vicinity, save to one young man of the name of Hugh Hutchison. This youth was their almost daily visitant, and from them he learned the nature of those principles for which they suffered; and he, who formerly sympathized with them from feelings of humanity, in a short time became one with them on religious grounds, and experienced the higher sympathy of Christian brotherhood. His heart being now knit to the sufferers in the bond of a common faith, he made their cause his own; and he conscientiously observed the sacred duty of visiting them in the day of their distress. It was his occupation to attend the horses and cattle that were grazing on the hill; and hence he had ample opportunity of meeting with them without interruption or suspicion. One day, as he was traversing the bent in the way of his calling, he heard the loud report of fire-arms on the top of the hill, in the distance; and not knowing what might be the matter, he hastened to the spot. When he reached the summit, and cast his eye along the mossy level, he saw a party of fierce dragoons on the spot where his friends used to conceal themselves; and Alexander Jamison, whom tradition names James Jamison, in full flight along the heath. On observing the scene a little more narrowly, he saw the other three weltering in their blood, shot by the merciless troopers, the firing of whose pistols had drawn him to the place. As he stood gazing in mute astonishment on the tragic scene, he was observed by the soldiers. He instantly fled; and the dragoons called on him to stop, otherwise he should instantly share the fate of those whose lifeless bodies lay stretched on the heath. The youth, however, paid no attention to their commands, but ran at his utmost speed for his life. To gain the heart of the impassable morass before his pursuers on horseback should come up to him he found to be impracticable, and therefore pursued his way adown the steepest part of the hill, in the direction of the Nith. His enemies still pursuing him, were fast gaining ground, and must soon have overtaken him, had not the thought occurred to him to seize one of the horses that were under his charge, and to gallop away with all the speed he could. This incident is similar to that formerly recorded of Thomas Hutchison of the same place; but then it does not follow that the incidents, though similar, are to be identified. The occurrence might easily happen in various instances—as it was in those times, and even at a much more recent date, the general practice of the farmers in the wilder districts, first to pull the shoes from the feet of their horses, and then to drive them a-field to graze at leisure, till their services were required for agricultural purposes. In this way horses must have been found strolling at large on every farm thoughout the country; and, on many occasions, may have been found serviceable in conveying the persecuted fugitives out of the way of their pursuers.

Hugh Hutchison being mounted on a stiff and heavy work-horse, had difficulty enough in preserving a safe distance before the well trained horses of the troopers. He crossed the river by a ford above Daljig, and then pursued his way along Dalricket-moss, and endeavoured to reach Dalec-cles-burn; but finding that his pursuers, in spite of all his efforts, were fast approaching, he changed his purpose, and passing over Auchengeehill, by the farm of Braehead and Rigfoot, he reached what is called the Lane. When he arrived at this place, the softness of the ground obliged him to dismount and flee on foot. The same circumstance, however, which retarded his progress on horseback retarded that of the dragoons. Having passed over the yielding and sinking ground on foot, he succeeded in hiding himself in the wooded banks of the Lane. The dragoons searched long and eagerly for their fugitive, but without success. The God to whose people he ministered in the day of their distress, and in whose sufferings he sympathized, shielded him from those who thirsted for his blood, and preserved him for further service. He remained in his hiding-place till the soldiers retired; and, with a feeling of security, he observed them marching along the heights of Lane Mark, and moving onwards to the defile of the Afton.

When all fears about his safety for the present were removed, he left his concealment, and returned to Daljig. With a heart full of concern and sorrow, he informed the family of what had happened; and in company with a number of others, he visited the scene of martyrdom, to ascertain the true state of matters. When Hugh and his party arrived at the spot, they found that three out of the four worthies had fallen by the murderous arm of their persecutors. When they were killed, they were left by the savage troopers unburied on the moss. This appears to have been the universal custom: they left the bodies of the slaughtered saints exposed on the face of the open fields, and if others did not choose to inter them, they might, for any thing that they cared, become a banquet to the ravens or the eagles of the desert. It is stated in the book of Revelation, that the murderers of the witnesses would not suffer their dead bodies to be put in graves; and truly those who shed the blood of God's saints so profusely on the moors and mountains of Scotland, acted a part akin to this. The sufferers, however wanted not friends to perform for them this last office; and there is no doubt, though it is not mentioned, that Hugh Hutchison and his companions dug their graves where they fell, and on the identical spot in the moss that had received their blood from the hands of their persecutors. Their place of sepulture is still conspicuous in the dark morass, where a monument was lately erected over their ashes, for the purpose of keeping in memory the tragical fate of these holy and devoted men, who sealed their testimony with their blood. Their resting-place is in the dreary solitudes and in the wilderness, where no man dwells; but their souls are in the paradise of God with Christ their glorious Head, for whose kingly supremacy they suffered the loss of all things, and for whose sake they counted not their lives dear unto them, that they might finish their course with joy. O ye who sought to obtain martial renown by slaying the people of God in multitudes, where now is your fame? Your names are a dishonour and a reproach among men, and will ere long be forgotten, or remembered only to be despised; while those whom ye vilified as the offscouring of all things, and oppressed, and killed, as pestilent and worthless men, are honoured in heaven, and virtuously esteemed on earth. Sleep on, ye bleeding bodies of the saints; sleep in your gory bed; sleep in the martyr's winding sheet; while ye sleep ye shall not be unattended; posterity will guard your lonely couch, and point out your dormitory to the inquiring stranger; and He in whose cause ye suffered, and in whose sight the blood of his saints is dear, will at length raise you from your lowly bed to shine among the sons of light in God's own house, and in his own presence throughout a whole eternity.

The history of the church of Christ has hitherto, for the most part, been traced in blood; and a goodly proportion of those, who are now in heaven, have suffered violent deaths for their steadfast adherence to the testimony of Jesus Christ. It is impossible to enumerate the thousands, nay, we may say the millions, that have suffered persecution for righteousness' sake. The first soul that entered heaven was the soul of a martyr, and since that time what innumerable hosts of martyrs, and confessors, and witnesses have, during the Pagan times and the reign of Antichrist, passed through the fires of a relentless persecution. It is supposed that Popery has put to death about fifteen millions of persons for the truth's sake, about six times the amount of the entire population of Scotland, reckoning it at two millions and a half. The whole population of Scotland murdered six times, how appalling the thought! And though the infidel historian Gibbon labours to lessen the number of those who suffered during the Pagan times, and to reduce it to a few hundreds, or, at most, to a few thousands, still there is reason to conclude that it could not be less than several millions. During the persecutions under the royal brothers, to which these gleanings refer, there suffered during the twenty-eight years, in one way or other, about eighteen thousand. Patrick Walker remarks, that, in the years 1684 and 1685, eighty persons were shot in the fields in cold blood, and this is merely a sample of what was generally occurring. The world cordially hates the church, and has many a time attempted to consume her utterly in the flames; for this purpose, it has eagerly administered the fuel, and Satan has brought fire from hell to kindle it. All that the policy of the devil, and the ingenuity of wicked men could devise, has been employed to harass and destroy the people of God. They have "had trial of cruel mockings and scourgings, yea, moreover, of bonds and imprisonments; they were stoned, they were sawn asunder, were tempted, were slain with the sword; they wandered about in sheep skins and goat skins, being destitute, afflicted, tormented; of whom the world was not worthy; they wandered in deserts, and in mountains, and in dens and caves of the earth." They were engaged in a great moral conflict, in a wrestling, not "against flesh and blood, but against principalities, against powers, against the rulers of the darkness of this world, against spiritual wickedness in high places." The conquest which they obtained infinitely outstrips, in grandeur and importance, the most splendid victories of those earthly warriors, the fame of whose martial exploits has made the world to ring from age to age. The wreath soon withers on the brow of the warrior, the palm fades and drops from his hand, and his glory is eclipsed by some succeeding hero; but those spiritual warriors, the great majority of whom lived unknown to fame, shall be had in everlasting remembrance before God. "Who are these that are arrayed in white robes, and whence came they? These are they who came out of great tribulation, and have washed their robes and made them white in the blood of the Lamb; therefore are they before the throne of God, and serve him day and night in his temple; and he that sitteth on the throne shall dwell among them. They shall hunger no more, neither thirst any more, neither shall the sun light on them, nor any heat; for the Lamb, which is in the midst of the throne, shall feed them, and shall lead them unto living fountains of water, and God shall wipe away all tears from their eyes."

It is probable that the friends who were killed in the moss had issued from their concealment, to meet the conventicle convened by Mr. Renwick, and that, in returning, they had been followed by the dragoons to the place where they fell. The individual who on this occasion escaped, namely, the brother of John Jamison, was afterwards seized by the enemy, and carried prisoner to Cumnock. No sooner did the report of this reach Hugh Hutchison, than he hastened to Cumnock, to visit his friend. The anxiety and solicitude manifested by him about the fate of Jamison attracted the notice of the persecutors, who began to suspect that he was one of the party. When Hutchison observed that he was noticed by them, he withdrew from the place, and betook himself to flight. This circumstance confirmed the suspicion of the soldiers, who instantly pursued. Hutchison, however, fled with winged speed over moor and moss, and at last succeeded in concealing himself in a cavern in the neighbourhood of Dalmellington, and escaped the breathless pursuit.

But to return to the first pursuit—when Hugh was so keenly chased by the troopers, at the time they shot the three men in the moss, it is said that he observed them from his retreat, passing over the heights of Lane Mark, and then descending in a straight line to Dalhanna, a small estate on the romantic banks of the Afton, about two miles above its confluence with the Nith. James Campbell was at this time laird of Dalhanna, and a warm friend to the covenanted cause. The approach of the dragoons was on this occasion observed by the worthy laird, who, suspecting their mission, left his house, to seek a hiding-place in the fields. There was, in the neighbourhood of his dwelling, a rising ground densely covered with broom, among the pliant bushes of which he hid himself. When the party arrived at Dalhanna, they inquired for the master of the house, and not finding him, they left the place, and began to ascend the hill close by the "broomy knowe," and so near his hiding-place, that he expected every moment they would discover him. And discovered he was, but by one who had too much humanity to disclose the secret. When the troopers were marching past the thicket, one of them, who happened to be straggling behind, observed Campbell in the heart of a bush, and, standing still, looked at him for a moment, shook his head, and passed on in silence. This soldier, it would appear, who was less hardened than his fellows, did not think himself obliged to make a discovery, where the party had made none, and left the honest man safe in his hiding-place, where God had been pleased to conceal him from the eyes of those who sought his hurt.

The dragoons pursued their way over the hills towards the farm of Cairn, beautifully situated on the slope of the range of mountains that line the sweet vale of the Nith on the South. At this place they came upon two men in a hollow among the green and flowery braes, engaged, it is supposed, in devotional exercises. The sound of their voices employed in prayer, or in the singing of Psalms, probably attracted the notice of the soldiers, and drew them to the spot. The names of the individuals were Hair and Corson. The circumstances in which they were found were enough to ensure their death, and therefore, according to the custom of the times, and the license of the troopers, they were without ceremony shot on the spot. They lie interred on the south side of the great road between Sanquhar and New Cumnock, where a rude stone pillar points out their resting place.

Hair was one of five brothers who occupied the farm of Glenquhary, in the parish of Kirkconnell, of which they were the proprietors. They were ejected from their patrimony, however, on account of their nonconformity, and forced to wander in the desolate places of the country. One of the five brothers was at the battle of Pentland, which circumstance would doubtless render the whole family more obnoxious to the dominant party. It is probable that Hair of Burncrooks, mentioned in a former chapter, and who effected his escape from the dragoons at Glen Aylmer, was one of the same family; and it is equally probable that Hair of Cleuchfoot, and William Hair of Southmains were, if not of the household of Glenquhary, at least related. In the old church-yard of Kirkconnell, which is situated at the base of the steep green mountains, and near the mouth of this romantic glen, there are to be seen in its north-west corner, six *thrugh* stones belonging to this family, indicating the successive generations that, one after another, have been gathered to their fathers. A lineal descendant of this worthy household is at present resident in the farm of Muirfoot, in the parish of New Cumnock, and warmly cherishes, as may be expected, the memory of his witnessing ancestry.

A similar incident to that now related occurred at Craignorth, an abrupt and magnificent mountain near the source of the Crawick, where two

Covenanters, named Brown and Morris, were killed by the soldiers. The incident, it is said, occurred in 1685, the year in which so many of the worthies were shot in the fields. Nothing further is known of them. Two small rivulets descend from the hill on which they were slaughtered; the name of the one is Brown's cleuch, and of the other Morris cleuch. Near the head of Chapman cleuch, in the neighbourhood of Nether Cog, lies a martyr; but neither his name, nor the names of those by whom he was killed, are known. More than five hundred persons were shot by the military in the fields, and therefore it is not to be expected that the names of all these individuals, or the circumstances of their death, could be recorded by history, or retained by tradition.

CHAPTER XIV.

Hugh Hutchison—Further particulars.

In the last chapter we left Hugh Hutchison in a cave near Dalmellington, in which he had taken refuge from his pursuers, and in which he continued till the danger was past. These men did not rush on martyrdom, nor needlessly expose their lives, for the honour of having it said that they died as witnesses in the cause of truth. They sought to preserve their lives by all honourable means as long as they could, thus proving that they were not actuated by a blind enthusiasm, but by an enlightened zeal. Life was as sweet to them as it was to other men, and therefore it was their care to preserve it; but then, sweet as it was, they were prepared to yield it up, at the bidding of Him from whom they received it. In the neighbourhood of his retreat, Hutchison had the happiness to meet with a fellow-sufferer, with whom he lived in concealment for a season. The name of his new associate was John Paterson. This man occupied the farm of Penyvenie, at the bottom of Benbeach, the ruins of whose dwelling-house are still to be seen on the right hand of the road from Cumnock to Dalmellington. These walls are the venerable remains of a cottage, which, in the suffering period, was a sanctuary to many of the people of God, and a temple consecrated to his worship. Owing to the severity of the times, however, Paterson durst not occupy his dwelling as formerly, but was obliged to seek a hiding-place in the fields. To his retreat in the "Tod Fauld," then, he conducted Hutchison, and here for a considerable time they continued in seclusion and security. Their intercourse in the day of common peril was doubtless such as became witnesses and sufferers in the same cause. Many a sweet hour did the worthies of these times enjoy with God and with one another, in the dreary caves and solitudes of the mountains, when their enemies foolishly imagined that they had despoiled them of all comfort and enjoyment whatever. Their foes might indeed expel them from their homes, and drive them afar to the lonely deserts, but they could not expel them from their rest in God, nor interrupt that spiritual intercourse with Heaven, which to them was sweeter far than all earthly comforts, or than even life itself. "Thy loving-kindness is better than life."

"He instantly rose from the table, and grasping his trusty sword, presented himself in the attitude of self-defence at the door."

p. 177.

From their place of concealment our two worthies descended, as frequently and regularly as circumstances permitted, to the farm-house by turns to their meals. One morning, when Paterson had stolen cautiously from his retreat to go to his house to breakfast, leaving his companion in the hiding-place till his return, a circumstance occurred which well nigh proved fatal to them both. It had been agreed on between Paterson and his friends, that when danger was apprehended, they should cry in his hearing "the knout's i' the corn." This watchword was unknown to Hutchison. It happened, on the morning alluded to, when Paterson was in his house at breakfast, that an individual at some distance, who saw three dragoons approaching, hastened to the lurking-place to give the preconcerted warning, not knowing that Paterson was at the moment in the cottage. Hutchison heard the cry, and not being aware that the words implied a sense different from their literal import, sprung from his concealment to drive the cattle from the corn-field. He no sooner issued into the open field than he discovered his mistake, for he saw three troopers marching with all speed towards the dwelling-house. He ran forward, with the intention, no doubt, of giving warning to his friend within, but durst not enter, as the party was close at hand: and, going past the end of the house, which intercepted him from the view of the horsemen, he plunged into the heart of a large willow bush, and there secreted himself.

Meanwhile the soldiers drew near, and John Paterson, who was at breakfast, observed their approach. He instantly rose from the table, and grasping his trusty sword, presented himself in the attitude of self-defence at the door. His affection ate wife, whom solicitude for her husband's welfare prompted to expose herself to danger, followed close at his back. The soldiers, in order to overpower their victim, made a simultaneous onset; but Paterson, with undaunted breast and powerful arm, brandished his glittering glaive above his head, and dealt his blows so lustily that he disabled two of his opponents, and laid them stunned, but not dead, at his feet. The third, a stalwart dragoon, yet unscathed, approached the valiant Covenanter, who so bravely maintained his position before the door, with a view to cut him down, and the more easily, as he was already exhausted by the stiffness of the conflict; but his wife, who, like a guardian angel, was hovering near him, hastily untied her apron, and flung it over the soldier's sword-arm, by means of which the weapon was entangled, so that Paterson made his escape without injury to himself. It was some time before matters were adjusted on the battle ground, and before the prostrate soldiers recovered themselves, and by this time the fugitive was beyond their reach. Meanwhile Hutchison was ensconced in the bush, to which the soldiers as they retired approached, and went round it beating it with their swords, as if they expected to start the timid hare from its lair in the interior, or to rouse from their nests the domestic fowls which in their raids they sometimes did not scruple to destroy or carry off. Hutchison lay trembling and perspiring, expecting every moment to be dragged from his retreat, and murdered by the infuriated soldiers on the spot. No incident, however, occurred; they left the place, and Hutchison remained undiscovered. When they were gone, and no further danger was apprehended, Paterson left his hiding-place, and returned with a throbbing heart to inquire after the state of his household; and having satisfied himself on this point, his next care was to search for Hutchison, whom he found in the heart of the bush. In this seclusion Hutchison chose to remain the whole day, and it was not till evening began to close in that he would consent to leave the covert. This caution on the part of Hutchison, was not without its reason, for the troopers sometimes returned when least expected. It was his intention now to return to Daljig in the evening, considering that his danger with Paterson appeared to be as great as it could be at home. At the earnest entreaty of his friends, however, he remained with them during that night; and on the morrow, as no apprehensions of the speedy return of their enemies were entertained, he agreed to assist his friend in the operations of hay-making. With buoyant spirits, while they inhaled the balmy breath of June, and with strong arms for labour, each with his scythe cleared with ample sweep the space around him, leaving the dewy grass mixed with its "fresh meadow blooms," in long files or *swaithes* of sweetly scented hay behind them. Shortly after high noon, Hutchison had retired to the house to dinner, while Paterson, in case of danger, kept his place in the meadow, mowing down the soft grass, close by the side of a field of tall standing corn that waved on the margin of a purling brook, at whose limpid waters the hay-makers frequently slaked their thirst.

In these circumstances the startling and warning cry was again heard; a clear, shrill voice proceeded from a distance, "the knout's i' the corn." Paterson rested for a moment on the staff of his scythe, and then darted into the heart of the growing corn, and hid himself in a deep furrow. The dra goons crossed the streamlet exactly at the place where the mowers had been employed, and perceiving the newly cut grass, and the scythes lying on the ground, they concluded that those of whom they were in quest were somewhere in the vicinity, and instantly proceeded to the search. The horsemen were accompanied by a few dogs, which they directed into the corn-field, for the purpose of making a discovery, if perchance any fugitive might be lurking there. The dogs, at the bidding of their masters, leaped into the corn, and traversed the field in all directions, as if fully aware of the design of the errand on which they were sent, and seemed to seek by their scent as keenly for men, as, in other circumstances, they would have done for game. Paterson heard the rustling of the animals, as they ran hither and thither among the tall and yielding stalks of corn near his hiding-place. Doubtless this good man prayed as he lay on the lowly ground, and besought the Lord to hide him, as in the hollow of his hand, from the fierce rage of his foes. And his prayer was heard; for though the dogs came close to him, and smelt his clothes, going round and round him, yet not one of them offered to bark, nor to give the least signal of a discovery, and they retired from the spot as quietly as if they had found nothing. Wodrow, when mentioning some very signal deliverances of the Lord's people, when they were almost in the very hands of their enemies, notices similar occurrences, and remarks, that the dogs, as he expressed it, *snouked* among the stones under which they were lying, and at the mouths of the caves in which they were concealed, without making any noise indicative of the presence of the fugitives.

As against the children of Israel of old not a dog in Egypt was permitted to move his tongue; so in these cases also, they were withheld from acting according to their natural propensity, when the slightest sound emitted by them might have proved fatal to the persons, in the pursuit of whom they were sent out.

When the dogs had issued from the corn-field, without having announced, by their barking, the presence of the individuals sought for, the troopers concluded that no person was there. Meanwhile Hutchison had taken refuge in his former retreat, the heart of the willow-bush, where he remained without discovery till the soldiers left the place. Thus were two honest men delivered twice on two successive days, in circumstances in which deliverance could scarcely have been expected; but, as was formerly remarked, "every man is immortal till his day come," and the Lord can preserve his people in the most perilous situation till their work be done, and all his gracious purposes respecting them on earth be accomplished.

This second attack by the soldiers, following the first so hastily, determined Hutchison instantly to abandon the place, and to return to Daljig. Accordingly next day he took leave of his kind friends, and proceeded to his home. On his way, however, danger beset him still, for in his lonely track he was encountered by a party of Highland soldiers who happened to be passing that way. As nobody escaped the notice of these marauders, whether on the moor or on the highway, they instantly stopped, and put to him their usual series of interrogatives, with the answers to which they seemed to be satisfied, and they allowed him to pass on.

It appears, notwithstanding what has been said to the contrary, that after the recall of the Highland host, which amounted to about ten thousand, and which, like a tempestuous cloud, burst with terrific fury on the west, or like a company of savages and beasts of prey let loose on the helpless peasantry, and whom even those who employed them were obliged, for their own safety, to dismiss, a goodly number of them was still retained for the iniquitous work, to accomplish which they were first brought in. On this subject, Patrick Walker makes the following remarks. "There are many thousands," says he, "yet alive who can witness, from their sad experience, that there were one thousand Highlanders in the month of March 1685, six years after Bothwell, who were sent to the south and west of Scotland, (it being killing time) to assist the forces—they being more swift of foot to run through bog and moss, hill and glen, to apprehend the sufferers, than the standing forces, who were turned fat and lazy with free quartering and strong feeding upon the ruins of the Lord's people, as also those Highlanders were brought to the west, to rob, and plunder, and to frighten people, more especially women and children, by their strange uncouth language, not knowing whether they were to kill them or to save them alive, which is a great aggravation of a judgment. And what great murder and robbery they committed these three months that they were in the south and west of Scotland, there is one instance among many that I could give, which I cannot pass. When they came south through the parish of Morningside, the curate there, Mr. Andrew Ure, informed them of worthy Peter Gilles who lived in that parish, who apprehended him, with John Bruce, who lived in the parish of West Calder; and when they went through the parish of Carluke, they apprehended William Finneson and Thomas Young, who lived there, whom the Laird of Lee's footman apprehended, on whom they exercised great cruelty. They carried those four prisoners to Mauchline, and apprehended one John Binning, waiting upon cattle, without either stocking or shoe, and took their Bibles from them, and would suffer none either to sell or to lend them Bibles, (the first four were my very dear acquaintances,) and hanged them all upon one gibbet, without suffering them to pray at their death, and their corpses were buried upon the spot." When the great body of the Highland soldiers were sent home, they returned loaded with booty, as if they had come from the sacking of a city, or from the plundering of a conquered country. Every article that was portable they took with them, although they lost much of it, if not the whole, in passing through the city of Glasgow, on their way to their native mountains.

Some time after this, Hutchison was made acquainted with a design which was formed by some of the country people near Cronberry, in the vicinity of Airs-moss, to rise in self-defence against the local oppression under which they groaned, and he resolved to assist them. On his way to the place he met with John McGechan of Auchengibbert, who informed him that the soldiers were traversing the country all round, and that it would be impossible to escape their vigilance; and that since the skirmish which had taken place at Carbelly, reinforcements had been received from Nithsdale; and on these accounts, the idea of ridding themselves of the evil of which they complained was, for the present, abandoned. This interview, it is said, took place on the romantic banks of the Lugar, above Logan-house. The classic Lugar flows past the pleasantly situated village of Cumnock—the theatre of Christian martyrdom; and in the burying ground of which place rest the ashes of that man of God, the venerable Peden. As the two men were discoursing together in fancied security and secrecy, two soldiers sprung from the thicket near them, with a view to apprehend them on the spot. The men fled, and the troopers pursued; but the fugitives keeping in advance of their foes, reached Auchengibbert in time to conceal themselves. There was in the house of Auchengibbert, as in the house of Glenglas on the Yochan, a place of secrecy, formed by means of a double gable, the entrance into which was through a small square hole in the inner wall, which was so closed, in ordinary cases, as to prevent suspicion. In this chamber, Hutchison and his friend took up their abode, and remained in perfect security and quietude during the time the soldiers were searching the premises; and by this means they escaped the vigilance of their enemies.

After this we hear little more of Hutchison for about three years, till the famous rescue at Bellypath. Bellypath is a narrow pass on the road to Muirkirk, a short distance from Cumnock. It is so formed, that a very few men could keep in check a considerable force. It was at this place, then, so formed by nature, and so much adapted to their purpose, that the country people in the vicinity resolved on the project of rescuing one Mr. Houston, and, probably, others with him. Mr. Houston, who succeeded Mr. Renwick, was apprehended in Ireland, and, being brought to Scotland, was escorted by a guard of soldiers on his way to Edinburgh to be tried. The Society people, fearing that he would share the same fate as the lamented Renwick, determined to attempt his rescue. For this purpose they assembled a number of their friends, among whom were Hugh Hutchison, John Paterson, and John McGechan. They secreted themselves at Carbelly during the night, and were prepared to encounter the party next day. Accordingly, when the soldiers, with their prisoners, arrived and entered the pass, the countrymen rushed forward, and, taking the troopers by surprise in the narrow defile, from which there was no escape, obtained an easy victory. Houston was rescued—several of the soldiers were killed, and some wounded—Hutchison and Paterson escaped unhurt, but McGechan was severely wounded. He was with difficulty conveyed to Auchengibbert, where, after lingering a while, he died of his wounds. His friends, to prevent the dishonour which they thought might perhaps be done to his remains, carried his body to the neighbouring farm of Stonepark, where he was interred; and the spot is pointed out by a suitable monument, which, a few years ago, was erected to his memory. He was a very worthy person; and Wodrow, in mentioning the incident of the rescue at Bellypath, calls him "a singularly pious man." The affair at Bellypath created much distress in the west; and the council at Edinburgh made a great handle of it to justify their oppressions. But it was too near the time which God had set for the deliverance of his church, for the enemy to proceed much further. It was the last year of the persecution—the famous 1688; and Hugh Hutchison, in a few months, was delivered from the terror of his foes. He lived many years after this, and was farmer of a place called Farthing Reoch. The descendants of Hugh Hutchison are still resident in the west, and are distinguished for their moral and religious worth. It is pleasant to witness the posterity of the good emulating the piety of a godly ancestry, and walking in the truth

CHAPTER XV.

John Paterson, of Penyvenie.

John Paterson, of Penyvenie, was born in the year 1650, ten years prior to the Restoration. When he grew up, he embraced the principles of the persecuted people, and followed their preachers in moors and mosses, at the risk of his life. The farm which he rented belonged to Logan of Camlarg, a man who, like most of the landed proprietors of the period, in order to save his estate, fell in with the ruling party, and submitted to their measures. One day, when John Paterson called at Camlarg, for the purpose of paying his rent, the laird remarked that the roads must have been very foul, as his feet were so much besmeared with moss and mud. In his simplicity John informed him that he had that morning come from Mayfield-hill, from attending a conventicle, which happened to be held there. At this Logan stormed, and severely reprimanded his tenant, pointing out the dangerous consequences that would certainly ensue, if the circumstance were to become known to the authorities. In those days of misrule and oppression, the lairds were made responsible for the behaviour of their tenants, and servants, and cottagers; and Camlarg distinctly saw the danger which threatened himself, if it should be discovered that any of the people on his grounds had transgressed the ecclesiastical law of the times. Logan therefore remonstrated with John, and stated that if he did not desist from the practice of attending field conventicles, he would be obliged, in self-defence, either to inform on him, or to eject him from his farm. In Paterson, however, he found a man of unyielding principle, and one who, having counted the cost, was prepared to sacrifice every earthly comfort, and even life itself, in maintaining what he deemed to be the cause of truth and righteousness. When he came home, he informed his wife of what had passed between the laird and him, and intimated his suspicions of what was likely to happen. His wife, who entertained the same views on religious matters with himself, was equally prepared to endure hardship in the cause of Christ. She encouraged her husband, by every virtuous consideration, to maintain an unflinching adherence to the principles which he had espoused. "If it be the will of God," said she, "let us suffer in well-doing, and, at the same time, let us make all necessary preparations for our defence, in case of an attack from the enemy." It was now obvious to John that more than ordinary precautions were necessary. He began to consider how, in case of a surprise, they might be able to conceal themselves from their persecutors, in places about the house and out-buildings; and it occurred to him that a small opening might be made in the wall, by which a passage might be secured into the adjoining office-houses, and from thence into the fields. Having, therefore, dug a hole in the gable through which one person at a time could creep with ease, and all other things being prepared, he, in order to conceal the aperture in the wall, placed before it a large wooden seat, called a *lang settle*, a piece of furniture very common in the old farm-houses in Scotland. In a day or two, as was anticipated, the soldiers paid them a visit; and Paterson observing their approach, made his way through the opening, and hid himself in a deep trench cut in the moss, not far from the house. The soldiers having, according to their custom, examined every place in which they thought there was any likelihood of his being hid, and not finding him, became very uproarious, and used very threatening language to his wife. They at last retired, and Paterson returned to his house unscathed.

Some time after this our worthy attended a conventicle at a place called Fingland, near the source of the Water of Ken; but the meeting having been apprised of the approach of a company of Highland soldiers, broke up, and Paterson pursued his way homeward. As he was proceeding onward, he observed two dragoons on horseback following him; but the ground being very soft and boggy, they made no speed, while he, being on foot, made his way lightly through the moss. It was his intention to conceal himself in some deep hag among the shaggy heath, till his pursuers had passed by. Accordingly, having passed the summit of what is called the "Meikle hill," he found a mossy furrow, into which he leaped, and lay close in the bottom. The troopers, however, had dogs with them, which they put on the scent, and directed them after him. The animals advanced over the broken surface of the morass, exactly in the line of his hiding place: he heard them approaching, and expected every moment when they would present themselves on the edge of the trench above him; but just when they were about to spring forward to the place where he lay, a fox jumped from his lair, in their very face, and bounded down the hill. The hunt commenced: the joyous dogs left their former scent, and stretched themselves out at their full speed after the fugitive reynard. The soldiers, like the dogs, oblivious of the principal object of their pursuit, followed in the chase, and passed Paterson in the moss, a few yards distant from the place where he lay. Hearing the hubbub, and not knowing what was the matter, he raised himself from his smeary couch, and peering cautiously over the edge of the deep hag, he observed the fox, and the dogs, and the soldiers, in full race down the heathy slope, leaving him far behind in comfortable seclusion. From the place where he had ensconced himself, he had a full view of the whole track to the door of his own house. He observed the movement of the party in the line of their route, till they reached the house at which they stopped for a short time, and then moved off in the direction of Dalmellington. He then cautiously left the height, and came home unobserved. Next day Logan sent for him, and informed him that he was publicly denounced as a rebel, and that a reward was offered for his apprehension; and that now he might consult his safety in the best way he could.

Matters having come to this pass, Paterson resolved to leave his house, and to take up his residence in Benbeoch Craigs, a place well adapted for concealment. From this situation he descended, as frequently as he found it consistent with his safety, to visit his household. One day, as he was preparing to go to his house, and had just left his retreat, he observed a company of dragoons approaching. He instantly retraced his steps, but was noticed by the troopers, who seeing him hastily ascending the hill, as if wishing to avoid their observation, concluded that he was either the man they were seeking, or some other equally obnoxious; and accordingly they rode after him. As he was climbing over the stone dyke which stood a few hundred yards from the bottom of the crags, he turned round to see what progress the horsemen were making, and perceiving the speed with which they advanced, he sprung from the wall, and ran to seek his hiding-place. In this place there are large masses of coarse granite, torn from the hill in the vicinity, and tossed to a considerable distance from the parent mountain, obviously by some powerful convulsion of nature. As Paterson in his haste was passing the base of one of these granite heaps, he fell, and tumbled into a deep and dark cavity underneath the rocky pile. Here he found a seclusion altogether unexpected, and much preferable to his usual hiding-place. When he fell into the cavern, he lay in utter astonishment at the incident; and being partly stunned, could scarcely persuade himself that it was not a dream. As he lay in darkness and silence, he imagined he heard the party, who were in search of him, talking and moving from place to place among the stones. In reflecting on the occurrence, he could not fail to perceive the special hand of providence, in thus suddenly and unexpectedly, covering him from the view of those who came to seek his life, and who, if they had found him, would without ceremony have shot him on the spot. When he considered the gracious care of that God in whom he trusted, his heart swelled with grateful emotions, and he often looked back to the time he lay under the rock as a season of the purest spiritual enjoyment he ever experienced on earth. It was a Bethel in which he found God, and so delightful was it as a place of communion with the Saviour, that he did not leave it till next day, when his anxious wife came to seek him, not knowing what had befallen him. John crept from the cavern, and met her in a transport of joy, and recounted his providential deliverance, and the outlettings of Divine goodness to his soul; and then the husband and the wife knelt down on the grass and prayed, and gave thanks to the God of their life. The incident at the granite rock was cherished in this good man's memory till his dying day, not simply on account of the temporal safety it afforded him, but more especially on account of that full assurance of his salvation which, during that night, it is said, he attained, and of which he made frequent mention on his death-bed.

Paterson was in raptures with his new hiding-place, which had been thus incidentally revealed to him; and he began instantly to arrange the interior, which he found capacious enough to contain several persons at a time, that he might render it a fit habitation for himself, and for any other wanderer who might happen to sojourn with him. It would be easy to make such a place very comfortable, by removing the loose stones and spreading the earthy floor of the cavity with dry straw, or with soft and scented hay, the common carpeting of the floors of the houses of even the nobles of Scotland in ruder times. The entrance to this re treat he contrived so to form that no stranger could easily find it, and thus the place was rendered so secure as to become a very eligible asylum in the time of danger. To this place he conducted the refugees that fell in his way, and it was here that he lodged Hugh Hutchison the incidents that befel whom, when he sojourned with Paterson, have been already noticed. Though none knew of his particular hiding place but friends, the people in the neighbourhood, by whom he was greatly respected, were ready to give warning to his family when danger appeared. Among others the farmer who lived on the side of the valley opposite to Penyvenie, agreed to give notice by crying across the ravine, the common watchword, "the nowt's i' the corn," and by this means he escaped on several occasions the vigilance of his enemies.

Some time after this he was in Galloway, at a place called Irelington, attending a conventicle kept there by Mr. Renwick. The meeting was held in the night season, under the serene shining of the bright moon, the night being preferred to the day to avoid discovery. As the company were listening to the preacher, from whose lips the words of eternal life distilled, like the refreshing dew on the grass of the field, a sound was heard in the distance, and anon there appeared a huntsman's dog in full chase, but without any apparent object of pursuit. The fleet and hilarious animal bounded several times round the outskirts of the assembly, and then darted in amongst the crowd. The circumstance attracted the notice of the congregation, and the preacher paused for a moment, and expressed his fears of approaching danger, especially as the dog seemed to have come from a distance, and not to be known to any person present. When they were beginning to deliberate on the propriety of separating, the warder, who had been stationed in the distance to give warning in case of the approach of the enemy, came running in breathless haste, to announce the appearance of a company of Highland soldiers, who were cautiously advancing in the direction of the conventicle. In an instant the meeting was dispersed, for it was now obvious that their gathering was known to the enemy. Paterson, with five of his acquaintances, David Halliday, John Bell, Robert Lennox, Andrew McRoberts, and James Clymont, took refuge in a barn in Irelington, and hid themselves in the midst of a quantity of wool that was piled up in a corner of the building, and by this means escaped detection.

But the danger consequent on his attendance on conventicles, did not deter him from meeting with the worshippers in the fields, or in the mosses, whenever an opportunity offered. He again attended a meeting near Little Mill, which gave serious offence to the Lairds of Carse and Keir, who complained of him to Logan, who sent for him and remonstrated with him on the assumed impropriety of his conduct, but without effect. Logan and his fellows, did not comprehend the principles from which such men as Paterson acted; they were themselves worldly men, and shifted with the religion of the times, from mere expediency, and to retain their earthly possessions; so hard is it for rich men to enter into the kingdom of heaven. The wealthy frequently possess far less independence of mind than the poor, for they have to guard their worldly interests and to change their opinions and professions to suit their interests; while the poor pious man, finding that the chief things which he has to protect are truth and a good conscience, acts independently of worldly considerations, not seeking to please men, but God. "Buy the truth, and sell it not," was to those worthy men, in the lowly walks of life, an injunction of the most sacred obligation. They indeed sold their lives, but they would not part with the truth. The great men of that time were mean and shuffling characters, compared with the upright and noble minded peasants, who, reckless of every worldly advantage, stood bravely by the cause of liberty, and high religious principle. They were men, many of them, in whose presence the truckling gentry of the nation were not worthy to stand an hour, and before whom they actually quailed, and from whose face they slunk away, vanquished by an oppressive sense of their own baseness.

Logan probably really wished Paterson well, although, for self-interest, and to ingratiate himself with the ruling party, he was obliged to appear displeased with him. He projected a sort of well meant, though silly scheme, with a view to bring our Covenanter, in some measure into the good graces of the neighbouring proprietors, who had conceived a very bad opinion of him. A number of the small lairds, whose grounds lay on the pleasant Water of Doon, had proposed to construct a dam across the stream, either for irrigation, or some other purpose, and a day was appointed when they and their dependents should meet for the purpose of executing the plan. Logan, who intended to meet with them, sent for Paterson, and asked him to go with him to assist in the operations, stating that he hoped his compliance would tend to produce a favourable impression on the minds of the gentlemen respecting him. John replied that if his attendance on that occasion was to be construed into a compliance with the measures of the times, he would sooner subject himself to any suffering, than move one foot in advance of another to lend his aid in the work. Logan answered, that all he wanted was his appearance there as a well disposed neighbour, ready to assist in any useful undertaking.

Having agreed to accompany the laird, John returned home, and informed his wife of what had passed, and how he had promised to go with Logan to help in constructing the dam on the Doon. His wife, who understood the temper of the men with whom they had to deal, suspected that a plan was laid to entrap her honest husband, who in the simplicity of his heart had consented to present himself among the enemies of that cause in which he was a sufferer, and attempted to dissuade him from carrying the matter further. John could not deny that his wife had reasons enough to suspect treachery, but he had promised, and therefore was resolved to perform.

On the day appointed, the party convened on the banks of the Doon, and Logan appeared with John at his side. They applied themselves vigorously to the work, and all went on smoothly and comfortably during the day. Towards night, however, an incident occurred, which broke up the harmony of the company, and threatened serious consequences. McAdam of Waterhead, in lending assistance to the workmen, lifted in his arms a large sod, and staggering forward with his burden, flung it with force on the watery embankment, from which it sent a muddy spray, which, reaching in a shower the place where Logan stood, bespattered his clothes, and especially his fine white stockings. This so enkindled his ire, that he broke out in furious and profane expressions against the individual who had unintentionally been the cause of so much annoyance to him. The matter was beginning to assume a serious aspect, and the wrangling of the parties was likely to issue in more substantial mischief, had not a peace maker been at hand. Paterson was distressed at the altercation, and much more so at the profane language, of which there was no sparing use made by the parties. His spirit was stirred, and he stood forward first as a reprover of sin, and then as a promoter of reconciliation. He was in the presence of men where danger was to be apprehended, on account of his well known non-conformity; and to dare to speak to them in the language of rebuke, might be regarded as a reason sufficiently strong to deliver him up to the military. But Paterson stood with undaunted breast, and spoke his mind freely at the risk of incurring the high displeasure of men already exasperated. He had a duty to discharge, and he was not to be deterred from its performance. He addressed himself particularly to Logan, whom he reprimanded as in the sight of God, for his daring and blasphemous expressions. The whole company stood mute and struck with awe, for there was a solemnity and majesty about his manner that quelled their spirits, and bereft them of power to reply. In the ardour of his address, and when he saw the advantage that he had gained, he drew, it is said, a Bible from his pocket, and read, with great gravity and impressiveness, the parable of the rich man and Lazarus, and, in his own plain way, endeavoured to draw a contrast between rich and wicked persecutors, and the pious poor whom they oppressed for conscience sake. What permanent effect his speech wrought on his auditors at Loch Doon, is not said; but the party separated quietly, and none ventured to assail the honest speaker, nor is it known that any injurious consequences followed. Paterson died so lately as the year 1740, at the great age of ninety, having long outlived the dreary period of persecution. His head was laid in an honoured grave, and his memory is still cherished in the locality where he lived. There were doubtless many interesting incidents in the history of this good man which tradition has not retained, but so many have been preserved as to keep his memorial alive, as a devoted follower of the Redeemer, and as one whom God cared for

CHAPTER XVI.

Capture at Glenshilloch—Rescue—Shooting at Craignorth—Roger Dun—James Douglas.

In the beginning of the summer of 1685, a year in which the persecution raged fearfully in the south and west, six men fled from Douglasdale, namely David Dun, Simon Paterson, John Richard, William Brown, Robert Morris, and James Welch. In their wanderings they proceeded southward, and sought refuge among the more inaccessible heights in the upper parts of Nithsdale. They concealed themselves in a thicket in a place called Glenshilloch, a little to the west of the mining village of Wanlochhead, in the parish of Sanquhar, and not far from the ancient farm-house of

Cogshead. This house, now a shepherd's cottage is situated in a delightful glen, and surrounded by lofty and green mountains. It stands not far from the edge of a precipitous brow, the base of which is laved by the limpid brook that traverses the glen, and pours its slender streamlet into the river Crawick. In the times of our persecuted forefathers, the place must have been a desirable retreat, as even now there are no regular roads that lead to it, except the solitary footpaths which here and there mark out a track for pedestrians across the hills. The family, which at this time resided in Cogshead, was related to William Brown, one of the wanderers who had taken refuge in Glenshilloch; and as the two places were contiguous, Brown made his way stealthily over the intervening height, and informed his friends of the circumstances in which he and his companions in suffering were placed. The sympathy of this household was easily gained, and an ample supply of provisions was conveyed to the men in the hiding-place. How long the party might have continued here among the dense brushwood during the warm days of summer is not easy to say, had not a strict search been made for them in all the glens and hills of the locality, in which it was suspected they had taken refuge.

The report had reached Drumlanrig that a company of refugees from Douglas Water had eluded the pursuit of the dragoons, and were somewhere concealed in the wilds between the Mennock and the Crawick. On this information, Drumlanrig collected his troopers for a vigilant search. He formed his party into three divisions, one of which traversed the lonely stream of the Mennock, another the pastoral banks of the Crawick, and the third pursued the middle route by the dark Glendyne. By this means it was confidently expected that the fugitives could not possibly escape, and more especially as no note of warning had been sounded in the district respecting the design of the persecutors. The six men who were lying among the hazel bushes, not anticipating any danger in their solitary retreat, had adopted no precautions in stationing a watch on any of the neighbouring heights to give notice of the approach of the enemy.

Drumlanrig himself conducted the middle division of the troopers; and having led them over the height in the north side of Glendyne, descended on the Water of Cog, and took his station on what is now denominated "the martyr's knowe," a romantic elevation at the lower end of an abrupt ravine, called by the shepherds the Howken. It happened while Drumlanrig and his party were on the hillock, that some of the dragoons who were scouring the adjacent hills in search of the reputed rebels, seized a boy who was returning from Glenshilloch to Cogshead, carrying an empty wooden vessel called by the peasantry a *kit*, in which were several horn spoons, a proof to the soldiers that he had been conveying provisions to some individuals among the hills, and they naturally suspected that the individuals of whom they were in quest were the persons. Under this impression, they carried him to their commander, who strictly interrogated him, but without eliciting any thing satisfactory. The firmness of the youth enraged Drumlanrig, who drew his sword with the intent to run him through the body, and would have slain him on the spot had not a second thought occurred, that by using other and gentler means he might eventually succeed in obtaining all the information he desired. With this design he caused him to be bound hand and foot, while he sent out the soldiers in the direction in which he had been seen returning over the hills. It was not long before the troopers, in descending the north side of the mountain, found the men in their hiding-place. They pounced on them as falcon on his quarry, and secured Dun, Paterson, and Richard, while Brown, Morris, and Welsh made their escape. The troopers having been so far successful in their object were seen returning triumphantly over the height; but ere they reached the rendezvous an unexpected occurrence took place which fairly routed the assailants, and accomplished the deliverance of the prisoners In the hilly districts, after a clear and chilly night in summer, the incident of a thunder storm after high noon is not unfrequent. When the sun has fully evaporated the dew, small dense clouds with bright edges begin to appear above the tops of the higher eminences, and, gradually, increasing in size, and approximating each other, form in a short time a dark and lowering mass of vapour, which soon overspreads the whole sky. An immediate thunder storm is the consequence, and so terrific sometimes is the explosion from the clouds, and the gush of waters from the teeming firmament, as to quell the stoutest heart. In these cases the fiery bolts falling incessantly on the hills, tear up the benty surface for a great space around, and the tumultuous descent of the waters, covering the green sides of the hills with a white foam, gathers into a torrent, which carries moss, and soil, and rocks promiscuously to the vale beneath, and forms all at once a trench adown the steep declivity, which afterwards becomes the channel of a mountain rivulet. It was with one of these hasty storms that Drumlanrig and his party were visited, and which had been gathering over them unperceived. When the dragoons who led the three prisoners were within a short distance of Drumlanrig's station on the Martyr's Knowe, the first burst of thunder rattled its startling peal over their heads. The horses snorted, and the sheep on the neighbouring heath crowded together as if for mutual protection. The rapid descent of the hail, the loud roaring of the thunder, like the simultaneous discharge of a hundred cannon from the battlements of the hills, and the flashing of the sheeted lightning in the faces of the animals, rendered them unmanageable, and they scampered off in every direction like the fragments of a fleeing army that has been signally routed on the battlefield. In the confusion, Drumlanrig himself, panic struck, as when Heaven bears testimony, by terrible things in righteousness, against the ungodly when caught in their deeds of wickedness, fled from the face of the tempest, reckless both of his men and of his prisoners, provided he could obtain a place of shelter. It is not said to what place he fled; but there can be no doubt that it was to the farm-house of Cogshead, which was scarcely half a mile from the place where he stood. When the soldiers saw their master retreating with such precipitancy from the warring of the elements, they followed his example, and let go the captives. The three worthy men stood undaunted in the storm, because they knew that the God who guided its fury was He in whose cause they were suffering, and though it was regarded with consternation by their enemies, it was hailed as a friendly deliverer by them, who were incessantly exposed to the pitiless storms of a wrathful persecution, compared with which the fierce raging of the elements was mildness itself.

When the prisoners found themselves at liberty, and being shrouded in the mantling of the murky tempest, they resolved to embrace the opportunity of instant flight. As they passed the Martyr's Knowe, they observed a person lying on its summit, apparently lifeless. This they found to be the little boy who had brought them provisions in the morning, and whom Drumlanrig, in his haste, had left bound on the spot. They untied him, and found that he was not dead, but only stunned with terror. Having raised him up, and informed him of what occurred, and directed him to keep himself in concealment till the soldiers should leave the glen, they went westward, and sought a retreat among the wilds in the upper parts of Galloway. The other three who escaped at Glenshilloch—namely, Brown, Morris, and Welsh—fled northward, and were intercepted by the party who were sent up the vale of the Crawick. Brown and Morris were shot at the back of Craignorth, where they lie interred in the places respectively where they fell, as has already been noticed in a former chapter. Welsh, in the meantime, made his escape, and remained in concealment among the Nithsdale mountains.

David Dun, one of the fore-mentioned worthies, was related to Roger Dun, a noted Covenanter, who lived in the higher parts of Ayrshire, and of whom a few notices may here be given. Roger Dun was born in 1659. His father, James Dun, a worthy man, was farmer of Bennet or Benholt, in the parish of Dalmellington, and was, with others, exposed to no small trouble in those trying times. Roger, when he grew up, and was able to judge for himself, resolved to share the fortunes of the Covenanters. It was soon known that Roger Dun had allied himself to the obnoxious party and therefore his ruin was determined on. A conventicle had been held at Craignew in Carsfairn, and Roger, with two of his brothers, attended the meeting. The report of this circumstance soon spread, and the dragoons were sent to apprehend all they could find returning from the place. They met the three brothers on their way home. Andrew and Allen were made prisoners, and carried back to Carsfairn; but what befel them is not known, for they were never more heard of. Roger, however, by a sudden and unexpected spring, eluded the grasp of the soldier who attempted to seize him; and bounding away, fled to a soft marshy place, into which the horsemen durst not venture, and made his escape.

After this, Dun sought a retreat in Dunasken Glen, a place about two miles from Bennet. One morning, as he was returning home from his hiding-place, he encountered, unexpectedly, a party of dragoons, who were sent out in search of him. He was so near them, that to attempt flight was in vain. In order, therefore, to avoid suspicion, he appeared to be as much at his ease as possible; and walking forward with an undaunted mien, he determined to accost the soldiers in a style that would have a tendency to direct their attention away from himself. "I think I can guess your errand, gentlemen," addressing the troopers in a familiar manner, "I am thinking you are in search of Roger Dun, who is supposed to be in concealment somewhere in this quarter." "It is even so," replied the commander of the party, "he is the very person we are in quest of." "Well," said Roger, "though I hate the name of an informer, yet I think I could direct you to a place in which he is sometimes to be found. See you yon shepherd's hut afar in the waste: bear down directly upon it, and see what you can find." "You are an honest fellow, I opine," answered the leader, "and we will follow your advice." The party then proceeded onward at full speed, and Roger, with all expedition, betook himself to his hiding place in the glen, which is said to have been beneath the projecting bank of a mountain streamlet. In this seclusion, where the hallowed voice of prayer often mingled with the soft murmuring of the silvery brook, he found a place of safety from man, and of communion with his God.

From the incessant harassings to which he was subjected, Roger Dun found it necessary to leave the district, and to retire to the lower parts of Galloway. When he was in the neighbourhood of Minigaff, residing in the house of a friend, who was favourable to that cause in which he suffered hardship, he had nearly lost his life by the hand of the enemy. The soldiers having made an attack on the house in which he lodged, two of its inmates were killed in defending themselves; and Dun, after an ineffectual resistance, fled, and plunging into the waters of a neighbouring loch, swam under water to a shallow place in the middle where grew several shrubs and willows, at the side of which he emerged, holding his head above the water, while the soldiers shot into the lake at random. Owing to his immersion, in the cold waters he caught a severe fever, which threatened to terminate his life, but from which he ultimately recovered. He lived till after the Revolution, and was at last killed at a place called Woodhead, by an individual who mistook him for another person whom he intended to murder; so that the worthy man, who had so often escaped the sword of the public persecutor, fell by the hand of the private assassin.

The scene of the following anecdote lies in the neighbourhood of the native district of Roger Dun. Near the head of the Afton, which springs from the dark and misty mountains to the south of the village of New Cumnock, was a hiding place among the brown heath, which was occasionally resorted to by the wanderers of the Covenant. The entrance to this retreat is said to have been along one of those deep ruts in the moss, which was scooped out by the torrents from the hills, which frequently descend with great impetuosity, after the discharge from a heavy thunder-cloud. Some of these trenches are deep and narrow, and the opening at the top is nearly covered over with the purple heather, which extending itself horizontally from both sides meets in the centre. In some cases a man can walk at his full height in these mossy water courses, without rising above the level of the surrounding surface. It was along this slippery ditch, that a few persons, seeking concealment from their enemies, had proceeded to the hiding place to which it led. The fact that a certain number of persons had concealed themselves somewhere in the locality, was discovered by a man of the name of Farquhar, who, though he did not know the exact spot which they had selected as their place of refuge, had yet noticed one of their party stealing cautiously in the dusk to a neighbouring house, to obtain provisions for his hungry companions. This man informed the commander of a company of troopers, who were either stationed in the district, or incidentally passing along the line between the garrisons in Carsfairn and Ayrshire, that he had observed something suspicious, and intimated his readiness to accompany him in the dark of the evening, to the house at which he expected the man would call as usual. The commander of the party, whose name, it is said, was Darnley, consented and led his troops privately to the place. Accordingly, as was anticipated, one of the Covenanters in hiding, was observed in the obscurity of the twilight approaching the house. He had come near without suspecting harm, but was soon made aware of his danger, by the whispering of voices and the appearance of men and horses, at a short distance from him. He instantly retraced his steps, and fled. Darnley and Farquhar pursued, and keeping on his track, came up to him as he reached the edge of the trench that conducted to the hiding place. The Covenanter, whose name was James Douglas, stumbled, and Darnley fell with him into the deep hag. The noise drew the associates of Douglas from their concealment, and they came in a body to the place where the two men were lying struggling in the bottom of the rut. They rescued their associate, and led Darnley, as their prisoner, to their rendezvous, and remonstrated with him on the impropriety of his conduct, pointing out the injustice and wickedness of the cause in which he was embarked, entreating him seriously to consider the danger in which his soul was placed, and exhorting him earnestly and affectionately to look to the Saviour for forgiveness. The kind treatment he received from them, and the good and salutary advices they gave him, made, it is said, a deep and lasting impression on his mind. In a short time he abandoned the cause of the persecutors, and embraced the principles of the Covenanters. He fought at the battle of Bothwell bridge, on the side of the Covenanters, and fell covered with wounds: and just before he expired, one of his former associates, who happened to pass the place where he lay, recognized him, and upbraided him with treachery in leaving the king's service, and connecting himself with rebels. With his dying breath however, he bore testimony to the uprightness of his motives, and to the goodness of that cause in which he was now a sufferer. "I do not regret," said he, "the step which I have taken; I die with a heart full of comfort, and in the faith of the blessed Redeemer of the world."

CHAPTER XVII.

Story of Alexander Brown.

Alexander Brown, the subject of the following sketch, is supposed to have been a native of the parish of Muirkirk, in which, during the heavy times of persecution, he rented a small farm, the name of which is not now known. He was cousin to John Brown of Priesthill, who among the saintly names that graced the period in which he lived, was without all controversy one of the most illustrious. Their places of abode were contiguous, and sweet and refreshing were the hours of their hallowed intercourse when they talked of Zion's affliction, and of the wailings of a bleeding church, whose glory the haughty oppressor was trampling remorselessly in the dust. These holy men, however, encouraged themselves in the Lord their God, and sought communion with the saints in prayer and Christian fellowship. Brown and his cousin of Priesthill, whose story is told with unrivalled pathos in the "Scots Worthies," took sweet counsel together when travelling into the heart of the remotest solitudes to hear the word of God, preached by the gentle Renwick, or the good Cargill, and others of the faithful witnesses for "Scotland's covenanted cause." It is not known at what period of his life the subject of this narrative was brought to a knowledge of the truth, but certain it is that he was a true and devoted follower of the Saviour. In "killing times" he was "in perils oft, in weariness and painfulness, in watchings often, in hunger and thirst, in fastings often." But the shield of a Divine protection was over him, and his deliverance in the most imminent dangers displays the overruling care of Him who was the comfort and salvation of that scattered remnant, whose blood flowed alike on the streets of the populous cities and on the sides of the desert mountains. Tradition has not named the year in which the following incident, productive of important consequences to Alexander Brown, took place. Claverhouse and his troopers were scouring the moorland districts in the upper parts of the counties of Ayr and Lanark, which from the beginning of the 'troublous times" had been the haunt of many a houseless wanderer. He had been informed that Brown who had hitherto eluded his vigilance, was at home unapprehensive of danger, and therefore might easily be caught. Claverhouse and his troopers were instantly in motion. Brown was at a short distance from his house when he descried he approach of the dragoons, and he was fully aware of their design in visiting his lonely dwelling. He knew that they saw him where he stood, and he found that he could neither flee nor conceal himself. He had reason to believe, however, that he was not personally known to his enemies, and hence he concluded that by employing an innocent stratagem he might perchance escape detection. Assuming therefore a cool and careless demeanour, he walked deliberately toward the advancing troopers, as if his business in the moor lay in the direction in which they were approaching, and as if apparently anxious also to gratify his curiosity by inspecting their military parade. This movement on the part of our worthy, tended to lull suspicion, and the coolness which he displayed so completely outwitted his wily foes that they applied to him for information respecting the object of their search. "Know you if Alexander Brown be within," asked the leader of the party. "He is not at present within, sir," replied Brown, with an air of indifference, "he went out lately, and I have not seen him return." "He *is* in the house," shouted a surly trooper, "and you want to conceal the fact." "What I tell you is the truth," retorted Brown, with some degree of warmth, "I know he is not within." This altercation was suddenly terminated by the stern authority of the commander, who imposed instant silence, and, with a voice that awakened the echoes of the glen, commanded the party to advance on the cottage, and, dashing the rowels into the sides of his black war-steed, was the first to draw bridle at Brown's door. In a moment the soldiers were at work, and made, as usual, a strict and unsparing search. Every place that could conceal a human being was closely inspected, but the object of their search was not to be found. Claverhouse, enraged at the disappointment, ordered his ruthless troopers to set fire to the entire farm-steading, and to reduce the whole to a heap of ashes. What moved the cavalier to this alternative was the belief that the occupant of the premises was lurking somewhere about the building, and he was determined not to leave the place till he had accomplished his destruction. But though the dragoons showed no favour to Brown, they had pity on his cattle, and drove them all to the bent, that they might be reserved for their own use afterwards. When the fire was raging along the line of the houses, the soldiers with their loaded muskets stood waiting for Brown, expecting every moment that he would issue from the conflagration to seek safety in the open field. In this, however, they were disappointed, and had the mortification to see the little *onstead* reduced to a heap of smoking ruins without having gained their object. Brown witnessed, from an eminence, to which he speedily betook himself when the soldiers left him, the entire desolation of his humble cot, and the spoiling of all his goods, but, like David, when he looked on Ziklag in ashes, and found himself in danger of his life, he "encouraged himself in the Lord his God," knowing that in heaven he had a better and an enduring substance.

After this, Brown, despoiled of all his worldly substance, but not yet bereft of his life, wandered for several months from place to place, till his enemies had abandoned the search as hopeless. When the noise made about him had subsided, and when the storm for the time being was hushed, he engaged himself as a shepherd at Carmacoup, a few miles above the ancient town of Douglas.

How long he was suffered to remain unmolested in this retreat, we have no information; but another severe trial was awaiting him. There were enemies, treacherous men, who, though not cased in armour, were nevertheless ready, for a sum of money, the wages of unrighteousness, to betray him to those who thirsted for his blood. Claverhouse being apprized of his retreat, marched with great secrecy and expedition to Carmacoup; and the only notice which Brown had of his approach was the array of his troop rushing along the heath towards the house which he had left a few minutes before. Brown, who had not forgotten the means of preservation which he had formerly employed with success when sought for by the enemy, prayed hastily for direction and help in the hour of his perplexity and peril, and then, turning from his path, he threw himself in the way of the dragoons that were advancing at a quick pace. On their coming up to him they halted, and rested on their steeds, smoking with perspiration and white with foam, and fixed their searching eyes upon him. Being prepared for the encounter, however, he met their scrutinizing glances without the slightest apparent agitation, and answered their questions with a simplicity and a tact which forbade the entrance, even for a moment, of the slightest suspicion. After a short confabulation with the stranger respecting Alexander Brown, and the likelihood of his being found at Carmacoup, Claverhouse hastened away, followed by his soldiers with their long cloaks streaming in the wind. In a few moments the trampling of the cavalcade, and the clashing of armour, died on the ear of Brown, who was again favoured with a deliverance when within the very grasp of the foe. Being now left alone, he fled over the moors and heights to a place called Hackshaw, about four miles to the north of Carmacoup, where he found a safe retreat in its wild ravines and deep morasses.

After lurking a few days in the Hackshaw, he removed to the farm-house of Cleuchbrae. Cleuchbrae, in the parish of Lesmahagow, lies about two miles north of Hackshaw, and is situated on the west bank of the Nethan, which rises near Cumberhead—a place famed as the resort of the wanderers—and falls into the Clyde at Crossford. In many places the banks of this dark whirling stream are exceedingly romantic. The rocks on either side are rugged, and clothed with wood. At Cleuchbrae, this stream, near its junction with the Logan, runs in a deep and narrow ravine, the precipitous sides of which are decorated by the stately oak, the fragrant birch, and the tapering mountain ash, which in summer waves its scented blossoms in the breeze, and in autumn is thickly studded with its gorgeous clusters of ruddy *rowans*, which furnish many a delicious repast to the crowds of sweet warblers which nestle among its leafy branches. Cleuchbrae, at the time to which our narrative refers, was tenanted by a worthy man of the name of Lean, whose door was always open to the lonely wanderer, who, for Christ's sake, had left all that was dear to him on earth. Here Brown met with a cordial reception. Lean's family consisted of four daughters; and to one of these, in particular, his visit was especially welcome. With the pious and hospitable family of Cleuchbrae, Brown had lived for years in terms of the closest friendship; but something stronger than mere friendship was cherished by him towards one of the household, with whom nothing but the precarious times in which they lived had prevented an honourable union. It was agreed on by the family, that, owing to the strict search that was now being made for him, Brown should retire to some place near them that afforded a more perfect concealment. Cleuchbrae was a suspected house, and being in the vicinity of Skelly-hill and Waterfoot, places which Claverhouse had often visited, and where parties of his dragoons for weeks occasionally resided, it was therefore deemed prudent that our wanderer should leave the house. The next care was to find a hiding-place, if possible, not far from the house; and, for this purpose, the steep and bosky sides of the Nethan were minutely searched, if happily a secure retreat might be discovered among its sheltering rocks; but no place suitable could be found. What nature, however, had denied, labour procured. Brown, assisted chiefly by his betrothed, excavated in the bank of the stream opposite to Cleuchbrae a cave, among the mantling bushes and thick underwood, which completely answered the purpose of concealment. The operations necessary to accomplish the design were carried on with the utmost secrecy, and for the most part in the night season. Brown quarried the stones and loose earth from the place; and she who had *volunteered* her services as a fellow labourer, conveyed, under the faint glimmering of the moon through the trees, the rubbish to a distance, and disposed of it in such a manner that nothing could lead to detection. At length the little cell was finished, and its entrance was so perfectly concealed by the shrubs and pendant branches of the larger trees, as to afford a high degree of security. In this asylum our worthy remained for two whole years; and she who had been his compan ion in labour, like a ministering angel, daily visited his lonely abode with a supply of provisions, accompanied with many an exhortation to maintain his constancy in that cause in which he was called to suffer hardship.

In the dark nights he frequently visited the hearth of the kindly family at Cleuchbrae, and, in case of a surprise by the enemy, he had his way of escape ready through the window of the apartment, which looked down upon his cave at a short distance from the house. During his stay at Cleuchbrae, however, no search was made for him, for none knew the place of his retreat except a few in whom implicit confidence could be placed. One of these few was John Black of Redshaw, in the parish of Douglas, a lineal descendant of whom is at present resident in Hazelside in the same parish, and one who inherits all the kindly feelings of his ancestor. Black had an interview with Brown, who had now been eighteen months in the concealment of the cave at Cleuchbrae, and expressed a wish that he should now leave his hiding-place and become his shepherd at Redshaw. Black, however, could not prevail with him to relinquish the place in which he had found so much security and peace, to expose himself again to the notice and fury of his enemies. After an interval of six months, his friend Black paid him another visit, and at last succeeded in drawing him from his retirement into active life, and with considerable regret he took his leave of Cleuchbrae. He was not long resident at Redshaw, however, before his troubles were renewed. Claverhouse was again in pursuit of him, and again he had nearly become the prey of the destroyer.

Early on a Sabbath morning, when he had gone

out to the heath to inspect the state of his flocks, he observed a company of dragoons on their way from Douglas sweeping over the hills before him, and rapidly advancing. His heart for a moment failed him, but his despondency was of short continuance. He committed himself to the gracious care of Him whose providence had hitherto watched over him, and shielded him from the vengeance of his enemies. 'Call upon me in the day of trouble, I will deliver thee, and thou shalt glorify me.' None but those who have experienced it, can conceive the confidence and ease of mind which, in perilous circumstances, the fervent utterance of the heart in prayer imparts. It was impossible for Brown to escape by flight; the troopers were near, and their horses were fleet, and he therefore determined to have recourse to his former plan of outwitting or outbraving the enemy, when no other scheme of escape was practicable. Accordingly he summoned all his fortitude, and turning round in an apparently careless manner, whistled aloud on his dog, that was lagging at some distance behind. When the joyous animal came frisking to his feet, he threw his plaid with a jocund air over his shoulders, and adjusting his broad blue bonnet on his head, began to chaunt in a lively strain one of our sweet Scottish airs, probably to the words of a Psalm adapted to his circumstances. The cheerful sound of the music attracted the notice of the dragoons, who conceived that no sober Covenanter could so profane the Sabbath as to employ on its hallowed hours the merry voice of the songster. The dragoons came up; it was a critical moment for Brown, life or death hung upon it. When they came close to him, however, though they slackened their pace, they did not halt, and riding slowly past, one of the party exclaimed, "That, at least, is not Alexander Brown, else he would not be singing songs on the Sabbath-day." The propriety of the remark seemed to be felt by the company, and they marched on without taking further notice of him. When the troopers had passed him, and were fairly out of sight, Brown lost no time in seeking a place of immediate concealment, and this he found in a deep moss-hag in the neighbourhood. The dragoons arrived at Redshaw in search of him whom they left behind them on the moor. They examined every place without finding their object, and, having ransacked the dwelling-house, they returned to Douglas. This was the last time that this good man was exposed to trouble from the enemy; for the Revolution, which took place soon after the occurrence now related, emancipated the nation at once from spiritual and civil bondage, and conferred on every man the perfect freedom of worshipping God according to the dictates of his own conscience.

Brown, when the danger was over, returned to sympathize with his kind friend at Redshaw, who on his account had sustained the spoiling of his goods, being reckoned a suspicious character when he harboured such men as Alexander Brown in his house. Tradition has not forgotten the fair maid of Cleuchbrae, who shortly after this, and in more peaceful times, became the honoured wife of our worthy Covenanter, with whom she was already united both in affection and in principle. After their marriage they took up their residence at a place called Little Redshaw. They had a family and both lived to a good old age. They died at Redshaw, and were interred in the ancient churchyard of St. Bride in Douglas.

www.ingramcontent.com/pod-product-compliance
Lightning Source LLC
LaVergne TN
LVHW011205110826
845150LV00006B/1327